To
Dr. Fadali,
I found this Brief Book
to be very interesting and
inspiring. I hope it will
be the same to you.
Syed Haque
- سيد هاشم -

His Throne
Was on Water

First Edition
1417 AH/1997 AC

His Throne
Was on Water

Dr. Adel M. A. Abbas

amana publications

Beltsville, Maryland USA

© copyrights 1417 AH/1997 AC by Dr. Adel M. A. Abbas
published by:
amana publications
10710 Tucker Street, Suite B
Beltsville, Maryland 20705-2223 USA
Tel: (301) 595-5777 — Fax: (301) 595-5888
E-mail: igfx@aol.com

Library of Congress Cataloging-in-Publication Data

Abbas, Adel M. A. (Mohammed Ali), 1931 (1350) —
    His throne was on water / Adel M. A. Abbas.
        p. (xiv, 134) cm. 23

ISBN 0-915957-62-0

    1. Koran and science. 2. Koran--Evidences, authority, etc.
I. Title
BP134.S3A227   1996
297'.1228--DC20

96-41514
CIP

Typesetting, layout, and printing by:
International Graphics
10710 Tucker Street
Beltsville, MD 20705-2223 USA
Tel: (301) 595-5999 Fax: (301) 595-5888 E-mail: igfx@aaol.com

TABLE OF CONTENTS

LIST OF ILLUSTRATIONS

INTRODUCTION

Although the Qur'an is not a book of science, scientific words, sentences, and sometimes even paragraphs are found throughout its text and call out for understanding or explanation. I have always been fascinated by such instances and hoped that one day I would be able to unravel their mystery. My attempt to do so started about fourteen years ago when I began to study modern sciences and build my medical experience. I soon concluded that any attempt to gather the scientific facts mentioned in the Qur'an, relate them to each other, and then work out possible scientific meanings would require more than just the use of a computer.

The Qur'an is a large text—6,243 verses contained in 114 surahs (chapters). This book deals with only 284 verses (4.5 percent). Many verses with scientific implications are not mentioned here, for modern science has not yet advanced to the stage where it can explain them. Social sciences dealing with such spheres as marriage, divorce, inheritance, contracts, witnesses, testimonials, civil and criminal law, morality, human relations, and taxation are also beyond the scope of this book.

The book's title is taken from the verse "His throne was on water," a verse whose splendor and scientific implication invite further reflection. The recent discovery by quantum mechanic researchers that outer space is full of virtual particles and antiparticles that materialize constantly in pairs may shed some light on this verse. This, together with the creation of the universe and the refashioning of the skies into concentric oval or ball-shaped layers, is illustrated on the cover. Such mysteries as space–time, humanity, the expanding universe, and the various stages of creation are addressed in the following pages.

The reader will find the chapter on Earth's creation very interesting. The author explains how God created Earth in layers, one of which (the lithosphere) carries the continents, remains in continuous motion, and floats on molten rock (the theory of plate tectonics); how God created "pegs" in the form of mountain ranges to prevent the plates' subduction zones from allowing the continents to disappear into the earth; how He created Earth in stages in order to stabilize it; and how He is going to dismantle it in reverse order at the end of the world. Many scientific facts are discussed, such as why seas do not flow into rivers, how atomic fractions are labeled and identified, and how supersonic waves are used for constructive purposes.

In addition, the creation of animals and humanity, the Qur'an's extremely accurate account of a human embryo's developmental stages, an individual's "imaging," and other issues dealing with the spirit, vital organs, expectancy, and fingerprints are discussed. The importance of animals to God as well as to humanity is also analyzed.

The scientific information presented in this book is directed to the ordinary reader. Therefore, I have left it to other authors to write in greater scientific detail on the aspects mentioned in this text.

During my research, I have sought advice from scientists all over the world. I am very grateful to all of them. I am indebted to the late Professor Doctor Abd El-Rahman El-Kordy, Vice Rector of Al Azhar University, Cairo, Egypt, who gave graciously of his time to discuss with me many facts and who also wrote the enclosed introduction. Sadly, he is not here to see the finished product

Dr Adel M. A. Abbas
Rotherham, England
December 1996

PREFACE

God created Earth. He spread it out and made it of different structures and colors. Some of it is rocky, some is muddy, and some is sandy. He made different specifications, capable of different purpose. For example, certain environments are best suited for certain crops. He caused fresh-water rivers to run through them and caused rainwater to fall on them so that plants and crops could be grown and thereby provide food for human beings, animals, and birds. He made it into layers upon layers, each of which has special characteristics from which we can extract metals and oil. He surrounded dry land with bodies of salty water, but whenever fresh-water rivers flow into them, the two types of water do not mix, for this would spoil their benefits for humanity. Earth rotates very fast, yet there is no disturbance or imbalance caused to either the land or the oceans.

He created the sun, which revolves at a rapid speed in its own orbit, and caused it to send its light and heat to Earth. From Earth's revolution come the four seasons and the accompanying climactic changes for every region. Some are hot, others are cold, and all have a function to perform vis-à-vis humanity, animals, and birds. He made the heat of the sun in such a way that it increases gradually during the day. He caused the moon and the stars to appear at night and endowed all of them with a specific task to perform in relation to Earth. The night and the day vary, for it is long in some places and short in others. He made the rain descend from the clouds and made it possible for human beings, animals, and birds to drink from it and for crops to use it to produce the food on which the planet's inhabitants depend. He surrounded Earth with the skies and created different worlds, worlds that He has mentioned but which the human mind cannot reach.

In His heavenly books, He revealed to humanity some of what surrounds it so that individuals can look and think in these worlds, all of which reveal the presence of a Creator, the Director of the universe. He created it, organized it meticulously, and has full knowledge of all its atoms and minute details. No human being can comprehend or acquire this knowledge of its details and particulars. If they could understand only a little of what He has created, they would return to Him, worship Him, and realize that He is the Strong Creator, the Supreme One that surrounds everything with His knowledge. This is why He invited His subjects to look and speculate on the universe and thereby increase their belief. In this book, we shall uncover some of these scientific matters that God has mentioned in His holy books.

Professor Abd al Rahman al Kordy
Former Vice Rector, Al Azhar University
Cairo, Egypt

بسم الله الرحمن الرحيم

قلبه لله الواحد وبسط و جعلم صلاته لو ... ولا ... وأوم
صمت ... بعلم ... ... وعمل ... وكنت كل قبضته نور ... متقابلة
لكل ذ ... وكل ... ... هذا هذا نص النوع الا أمر ...
ولا استفاد ... ... وأ انوار ... مبنية ... كل نوع منها ...
لموضوعات معينة وأ ... من الأنوار ... ... وأ ...
ا ... مطار الته ... ...
لما في الانسان والحيوان و ... الطير و جعلها طبعا ... نينو
يعلم نوره بعضه لكل طبقة فصا ... نينو ... ...
... معارهم وبين ... وأحاط اليابس بالبحار الملح ومنها
... ... لا بد ... فلا انا ... طع ... ... يلحظ على ... ...
... ... صنائع البشر ... وهي ... ... صول نفسك دولة ...
... هذا الامير ... المطراب وأ فعلاد ... اليابس أو البحار
وفلكم الشمس ... ...
مسرعة محدثة ... ... جد العصور بالأربع
... ... في كل سلطنة ... ... هار وبعضها بارد وكلا منها دفين
نو ... ... الانسان والحيوان والطير وجعل ... ...
... ... وصا ... ... وتكل ... ... عمل نور ... بالنهم
... ... يختلف الليل والنهار لهم ... وتكرا ... ... وجعل
ا ... ... الانسان والحيوان ... ...
... ... العالم وأطا ... ...
با ... ... وعلوم ... ...
ا ... ...

Translation of the preface by the late Professor Abd al Rahman al Kordy, former Vice Rector of Al Azhar University, Cairo, Egypt

CHAPTER ONE

TIME: THE FOURTH DIMENSION AND RELATIVITY

Time and Its Measurement

The awareness of time is an important facet of human nature. Unlike other living creatures, each human being is aware that his/her life can be cut short at any moment and that full growth is followed by decay and eventual death.

Since the earliest days, people have tried to measure time. Shadow clocks and sundials were known as early as (roughly) 3500 BCE. They consisted of a vertical stick or pillar (*gnomon*) that indicated the time of day by the length of its shadow. An Egyptian shadow clock of green schist, dating from about the eighth century BCE and consisting of a straight base with a raised cross-piece at one end, has survived until our own time. The base is inscribed with a scale of six time divisions. When placed in an east-west direction with its cross-piece pointed toward the east in the morning and the west in the afternoon, a shadow is cast on the base and indicates the time. This idea was transmitted to the Greeks and the Romans. The Muslims later improved upon the models by using the principles of trigonometry. In addition, they produced manuals on how to construct hour lines on cylindrical, conical, and other surfaces and are credited with being the first to introduce hours of equal length, especially for astronomical purposes.

The ancient Egyptians invented water clocks and clepsydras to record time during the night or when the sun was obscured. Existing examples dating from about 1400 bce consist of bucket-shaped vessels from which water escapes through a small hole at the base. Uniform scales of time were marked on the inside—one for each month—to allow for the different seasonal lengths of Egyptian hours, and its slopin sides were designed to regulate the pressure of outflow from these clocks. Eventually, such clocks were introduced into the classical world.

After that came sand-glass and then mechanical clocks. The Clock of Damascus was described in the thirteenth century. Weight-driven clocks have been known since the fourteenth century (the first such clock, which chimed off each hour, was erected in 1335 in Milan, Italy). In England, the Salisbury Tower Clock dates from 1386 while the one in Rouen, France, dates from 1389. Spring-driven clocks were introduced in the fifteenth century, and the pendulum clock was developed by Galileo in 1582.

Initially, medical professionals used clocks to count their patients' pulse. In 1656, the Dutch astronomer and physicist Christiaan Huygens became the first person to use pendulums in clocks. William Clement, an English clock-maker, introduced the long second pendulum in 1670. The recoil escapement was invented in England by Robert Hooke in 1660, and the double three-legged gravity escapement, the most famous example of which is London's Big Ben, was invented and introduced by Lord Grimthorpe in 1859. Electric clocks, which are powered by an electric current instead of a weight or a spring, represented the next advance in the measurement of time. Synchronous electric motor clocks were popular in 1918. By 1929, quartz crystals oscillating at frequencies of 100,000 Hz (cycles per second) and having an accuracy rate of 10^{10} were being used for clocks.

The chronometer, a time-keeping device of great accuracy, was of particular usefulness for determining longitude at sea. John Harrison, a self-taught English carpenter, won a prize, in 1714, of £20,000 from the British government for his chronometer, which could determine a ship's longitude within thirty nautical miles at the end of a six-week voyage. The chronometer had to remain horizontal regardless of the ship's inclination.

The first patent for the self-winding pocket watch was taken out in London in 1780. The first electronic watch was introduced in 1953. Atomic clocks utilize and register oscillations that occur in individual atoms. The caesium clock was first investigated in the United States in 1952. The second caesium clock is installed at the National Physical Laboratory at Teddington near London. It is so precise that any discrepancy is equivalent to 1 second every 1,000 years. In addition, it is used to calculate the Greenwich Mean Time (GMT), which served for many years as the basis of standard time throughout the world and has been kept 10 seconds behind International Atomic Time (IAT). GMT is the local mean solar time of the longitude 0° of Greenwich, England. Also known as Universal Time (UT), it is based on the Earth's rotation, which is not quite constant. In 1972, UT was replaced by Coordinated Universal Time (CUT), which, in turn, is based on Uniform Atomic Time. In 1986, the term "Greenwich Mean Time" was changed to "CUT." However the Greenwich meridian, adopted 1884, remains the longitude from which all longitudes are measured and from which the world's standard time zones are calculated.

Standard time was agreed upon in 1884 during a meeting in Washington, DC, that was attended by twenty-seven nations. The present system employs twenty-four standard meridians of longitude (lines running from the north to the south poles at right angles to the equator) that are fifteen degrees apart and use Greenwich, England, as their starting point. Time differs by one hour for each fifteen degrees and four minutes for every degree.

Solar time is measured by Earth's rotation in relation to the sun. Sidereal time is the measurement of Earth's rotation relative to the stars and is used by astronomers to locate celestial bodies. Ephemeris Time (ET) was introduced in 1950 as a more reliable basis for measurement, as Earth's rotation was found to change. It is calculated from the orbital motion of the planets and is independent of Earth's rotation. In practice, the moon is generally used because of its rapid orbital motion. Very accurate positions of the moon are obtained visually by observing the occultations of various stars (an occultation is the passage of the moon across the line of sight to a star, which causes the star to vanish for a short time). The difference between ET and Mean Solar Time amounts to a few tenths of seconds per century. Ephemeris Time has now been replaced by Atomic Time.

This is how much humanity values time. Ever since the earliest known civilizations, individuals have sought to measure it and to obtain even more sophisticated measurements as human knowledge and technology developed.

The Fourth Dimension

People have always recognized past, present, and future time. The idea of going backward and forward in time was mentioned by some writers and philosophers during the eighteenth and nineteenth centuries. No one can be certain whether such narrators were influenced by the holy books or were simply letting their imaginations run wild. Certainly one scientist, Isaac Newton, who built on the concept of "Galilean space and time," maintained that time and space are absolute and that time never varies with the change of place in space.

Newton's theories remained undisputed until Henri Poincaré, a famous French mathematician, refuted the theory of absolute time and space by developing his theory of relativity in 1904. One year later, Albert Einstein published his paper on special relativity. Both scientists postulated that time, far from being absolute, actually varies for different objects in the universe. This theory was proved by Einstein and others over the following years. His statement that "God is not playing at dice" shows his sincere belief that the world was not created by chance.

However, credit must be given to the Dutch physicist Hendrick Antoon Lorentz (1853-1928), a pioneer in formulating relations between electrical magnetism and light. He was also the first to postulate the concept of electrons and to describe what is now known as the Lorentz contraction, namely, the contraction in dimensions (or time scale) of a body moving through the ether with a velocity approaching that of light, relative to the frame of reference (Lorentz frame) from which measurements are made. His concept of space and time was a forerunner of Einstein's special theory of relativity. He shared the Nobel prize in physics for the explanation of the Zeeman effect change in the spectrum lines of a magnetic field.

Einstein was influenced in many ways by Poincaré, who was considered by Sir Edmund Whittaker as the real founder of the theory of special relativity. Einstein, the student, attended Poincaré's conferences and later used his formulae of integral invariants and astronomical perturbation for his own advanced calculations. Poincaré was a distinguished mathematician and made many bold and inspired statements, such as "suppose that one night all the dimensions of the universe became a thousand times larger."

The concept of relativity was asserted by God almost 1400 years ago. The Qur'an came with a full explanation of the variable nature of time and place. It proved that neither of these dimensions is, in fact, absolute. Time is shown to be variable in several verses of the Qur'an, i.e., "everything will return to him, on a day whose length will be as a thousand years of your counting" This shows the relativity of time between humanity and God.

He rules everything from the heavens to the earth. In the end, everything will return to him, on a day whose length will be as a thousand years of your counting. (32:5)

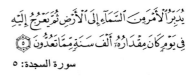

This simple and plain statement makes it clear that time is variable between our Earth and our observers in the universe. In another verse, just as impressive, it is stated that "one day with God is as a thousand years of your counting."

They ask you to bring the punishment quickly. God will keep His promise. Truly, one day with God is as a thousand years of your counting. (22:47)	وَيَسْتَعْجِلُونَكَ بِالْعَذَابِ وَلَن يُخْلِفَ اللَّهُ وَعْدَهُۥ وَإِنَّ يَوْمًا عِندَ رَبِّكَ كَأَلْفِ سَنَةٍ مِّمَّا تَعُدُّونَ ﴿٤٧﴾ سورة الحج: ٤٧

This statement was made to people who were asking Prophet Muhammad when the Day of Judgment would come. God stated that such an event appears near to Him although people think it will never come. This demonstrates the relative value of time to God and humanity. However, it must be emphasized that the word "with" God indicates that the thousand years is in no way the time "of" God, but in fact only a time "with" Him. It could simply mean that this is the time of our observations in the universe.

There is also evidence that time is changeable. Not only can one day with God be equal to a thousand years of our counting, but on another occasion it can be equal to fifty thousand years. Variations of time between God and humanity is an early spiritual demonstration of the fourth dimension: that of time.

The angels and the spirit ascend to Him during a day which is as fifty thousand years. (70:4)	تَعْرُجُ الْمَلَـٰٓئِكَةُ وَالرُّوحُ إِلَيْهِ فِي يَوْمٍ كَانَ مِقْدَارُهُۥ خَمْسِينَ أَلْفَ سَنَةٍ ﴿٤﴾ سورة المعارج: ٤

It is now accepted that time is variable in the different spaces of the universe and that each place has a different frame of reference (i.e., dimensions). It is also known that the position of places in the universe decides their relative timing. There is strong evidence of these facts from the Qur'an. It is known that, on the Day of Doom, our planet and the skies will be subjected to radical changes and will be exchanged for different ones.

When the sky is rent asunder and harkens to God's (command), as it must do. And when the earth is flattened and expels what is within it and becomes empty and harkens to God's (command), as it must do, (then will the full Reality appear). (84:1-5)	إِذَا السَّمَآءُ انشَقَّتْ ﴿١﴾ وَأَذِنَتْ لِرَبِّهَا وَحُقَّتْ ﴿٢﴾ وَإِذَا الْأَرْضُ مُدَّتْ ﴿٣﴾ وَأَلْقَتْ مَا فِيهَا وَتَخَلَّتْ ﴿٤﴾ وَأَذِنَتْ لِرَبِّهَا وَحُقَّتْ ﴿٥﴾ سورة الانشقاق: ١-٥

Some are probably unaware that a "new Earth" will be prepared for the Day of Judgment.

One day the earth will be changed into a different earth, as the heavens will also be, and (humanity) will come forth before God, the One, the Supreme. (14:48)

يَوْمَ تُبَدَّلُ ٱلْأَرْضُ غَيْرَ ٱلْأَرْضِ وَٱلسَّمَوَٰتُ
وَبَرَزُوا۟ لِلَّهِ ٱلْوَٰحِدِ ٱلْقَهَّارِ ﴿٤٨﴾

سورة ابراهيم: ٤٨

Our existing Earth is about 93 million miles distant from the sun and needs exactly one year to complete its elliptical orbit. Earth is kept near the sun by the pull of gravity and is kept from being drawn into the sun by its own high speed (roughly 66,600 miles per hour). The position of the "new Earth" is unknown, yet we are informed of its timing. The Day of Judgment on this new Earth will be equal to 50,000 years of our counting.

The angels and the spirit ascend to Him during a day which is as fifty thousand years. (70:4)

تَعْرُجُ ٱلْمَلَٰٓئِكَةُ وَٱلرُّوحُ إِلَيْهِ فِى يَوْمٍ كَانَ
مِقْدَارُهُۥ خَمْسِينَ أَلْفَ سَنَةٍ ﴿٤﴾   سورة المعارج: ٤

These figures must have been perplexing. It is now known that all objects in the sky are very distant from us. In fact, such distances are measured in multiples of the speed of light (186,300 miles per second). As the sun is 300,000 times closer to Earth than the nearest star to Earth, distances to the stars are usually referred to in minutes, months, or years of light. God has explained in the succeeding verses that the Day of Judgment is seen by people as far off although He sees it as near.

They see the (day) as far off, while We see it as (quite) near. (70:6-7)

إِنَّهُمْ يَرَوْنَهُۥ بَعِيدًا ﴿٦﴾ وَنَرَىٰهُ قَرِيبًا ﴿٧﴾

سورة المعارج: ٦-٧

This simply explains in words, rather than figures, that neither time nor space is absolute and that both dimensions are variable. If the variation of time and place had been appreciated from early times, the concept of relativity would have been developed many years ago. Such early progress would have probably brought forward our civilization. Without going into detailed mathematics, one can appreciate that an observer in the universe, at a fraction of a time equal to a thousand years of ours, could easily see billions of people born, live, and die during this period. Therefore, it is not surprising that God can see the past, present, and future.

CHAPTER TWO

THE CREATION OF THE UNIVERSE

The Universe of the Scientists

Until the end of the nineteenth century, the universe was thought to have existed as seen today, namely, eternal and unchanging. One can imagine that God created an eternal and unchanging universe at any time in the past. However, the theory of general relativity and the fact that galaxies are receding from Earth, as evidenced by the "red shift" of their spectrum, caused scientists to consider the possibility that the universe, far from being static, was actually expanding and moving away.

This has now been accepted as fact. Such an expansion gave rise to the suggestion that there must have been a beginning or, as formulated in accepted scientific literature, a "big bang." An expanding universe suggests that there must be physical reasons why there has to be a beginning, but the theory of general relativity cannot explain how the universe began. From a fixed external space and time, which has always been empty, the universe, for an unknown reason, was nucleated as a specific point and caused a "big bang" that it blew apart (fig. 1). When space and time appeared, the actual point was a singular point at which all the laws of mathematics and physics broke down and could not be applied.

In 1965, Roger Penrose studied the way light cones behave in general relativity and, given that gravity is always attractive, showed that a star collapsing under its own gravity would be trapped in a region whose surface would eventually shrink to zero. Just as the region's surface shrinks to zero, so must its volume. All of the matter in the star would be compressed into a region of zero volume, which would cause the density of matter and the curvature of space–time to become infinite. In other words, one has a singularity contained within a region of space–time, a phenomenon that has been termed a "black hole."

Professor Stephen Hawking of the University of Cambridge, who was a research student at this time, believed that if one reversed the direction of time in Penrose's theorem and thereby transformed a collapse into an expansion, the conditions of his theorem would still hold. He postulated that what happens to stars could help explain the beginning and end of the universe. He thought that if one were to reverse the sequence of time, one could imagine the universe as a gigantic star in the process of collapse.

Penrose explained that a dying star, whose mass would be much greater than the sun's, would eventually exhaust its nuclear fuel. Its core would cool, contract, and then begin to collapse under the enormous weight of the outer layer. This would be effected by its own gravity. Eventually, it would shrink to singularity, which is defined as a point of infinite density and zero size. At this stage, it is referred to as a black hole or an unseen star (fig. 2). The black hole stage was predicted by the theory of general relativity.

Nothing can escape from a black hole. Its radius is called the "event horizon" or the "Schwarzschild Radius," after the German astronomer Karl Schwarzschild, who predicted the existence of invisible stars in 1907. For a body to escape the gravitational dominance of a black hole, it must have a speed greater than the speed of light, which is impossible. A black hole can have any size depending upon its age, mass, and angular momentum.

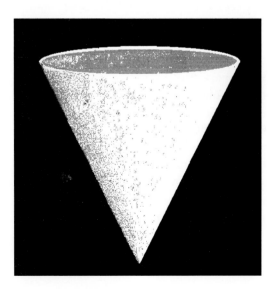

Figure 1: *Diagram of the beginning of time and space according to the Big Bang theory. It possesses a point of singularity where laws of mathematics and physics cannot be applied.*

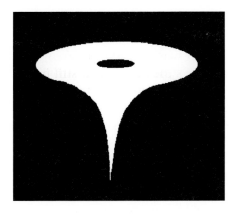

Figure 2: *A black hole. It is not completely black, however, as it emits gamma rays and x-rays.*

If an astronaut were to enter a black hole, he would be entering a point of no return. As he approached the center, the curvature of the space–time "whirlpool" would continue to increase and eventually become infinite at the singularity's central point. Under such conditions, no outside observer would be able to make contact with the astronaut in question. This latter individual, in turn, would be compressed to near-infinite density, losing in the process virtually every property of identity except mass, electric charge, and angular momentum.

In the long history of the universe, many stars must have exhausted their nuclear fuel and collapsed in upon themselves. The number of black holes may be greater than that of visible stars—about 100 billion in our galaxy alone. There is evidence of a large black hole in our galaxy's center.

The theory of general relativity predicts a certain path for each particle. According to quantum mechanics, there is an element of chance or uncertainty. A particle does not have a single path through space and time, for there is an uncertainty principle according to which a particle's exact position and velocity can never be known. Hawking studied the effect of quantum mechanics on particles near a black hole and found that particles could escape as residual radiation. This discovery indicated that black holes were not as black as was thought originally. In a black hole, negative energy particles are created and radiation can escape.

According to quantum mechanics, space is filled with virtual particles and anti-particles that are constantly materializing in pairs, separating, coming together again, and eventually annihilating each other. In the presence of a black hole, one member of this pair may fall into the black hole and leave the other member without a partner to be annihilated. The forsaken particle would appear as radiation emitted by the black hole. Black holes evaporate at varying rates until they disappear in a giant explosion. According to Hawking, an astronaut in a black hole would come back to the universe in the form of radiation. In other words, he would be recycled.

Hawking believes that when the universe stops expanding, it will begin to contract, as this is the usual process for a star. However, time will not reverse direction. The universe will have two possible directions: continued and eternal expansion or collapse and extinction in a "big crunch." He believes it will come to an end.

How the universe was made, what is happening in it, and how it will end has been the subject of many studies. None of the resulting theories are simple enough for ordinary people to understand. No matter how modest the scientists, they have been unable to make the subject simple enough for everyone to appreciate. Even when one feels that he/she has reached the high point of human reasoning, he/she is still very far from the truth. What is known today? A universe, created at a point of singularity that does not comply with mathematical or physical laws, started with a "big bang" and, possibly, may finish with a "big crunch." Some scientists replace the point of singularity with a rounded or curved end (fig. 3) through the use of mathematics based on the imaginary direction of time. This bowl-shaped structure, which would obey mathematical and physical laws, would not present the facts, for it is a self-consistent structure that cannot be created or destroyed and is based on an imaginary direction of time.

Figure 3: *A universe that has no point of singularity. The laws of mathematics and physics could be applied. It is self-contained and does not necessarily need a creator.*

The Universe as Suggested by the Qur'an

Although the Qur'an is not a book of science (16:64), it contains many references to scientific facts. These were given in a manner designed to suit the minds and education of the people at that particular point in time.

And We sent down the Book so you could make clear to them those things in which they differ and that it should be a guide and a mercy to those who believe. (16:64)	وَمَآ أَنزَلۡنَا عَلَيۡكَ ٱلۡكِتَٰبَ إِلَّا لِتُبَيِّنَ لَهُمُ ٱلَّذِي ٱخۡتَلَفُوا۟ فِيهِ وَهُدًى وَرَحۡمَةً لِّقَوۡمٍ يُؤۡمِنُونَ ۝ سورة النحل: ٦٤

It is unwise to dismiss such facts or treat them lightly. In the last chapter, variation between God and man was discussed and it was thought to be an early spiritual demonstration of time (the fourth dimension). Humanity had to wait for Poincaré and Einstein to unveil the secrets of time. The creation of the universe has been revealed in the Qur'an. When all of the facts are put together, a clear picture of how it began and where it is going is revealed. A brief summary of the facts, along with their possible scientific interpretations, are presented in this chapter.

God is the first, the last, the evident, and the innermost. Nobody can quantify such an assertion mathematically, cosmologically, or even by means of quantum mechanics.

He is the First and the Last, the Evident and the Hidden. He has full knowledge of everything. (57:3)	هُوَ ٱلۡأَوَّلُ وَٱلۡأَخِرُ وَٱلظَّٰهِرُ وَٱلۡبَاطِنُ وَهُوَ بِكُلِّ شَيۡءٍ عَلِيمٌ ۝ سورة الحديد: ٣

He created the heavens and Earth in six days, and His throne was upon the waters.

He created the heavens and the earth in six days, and His throne was upon the waters, that He might try you to see which of you is best in conduct. If you were to say to them, "We shall be raised up after death," the unbelievers would reply, "This is only obvious sorcery." (11:7)	وَهُوَ ٱلَّذِي خَلَقَ ٱلسَّمَٰوَٰتِ وَٱلۡأَرۡضَ فِي سِتَّةِ أَيَّامٍ وَكَانَ عَرۡشُهُۥ عَلَى ٱلۡمَآءِ لِيَبۡلُوَكُمۡ أَيُّكُمۡ أَحۡسَنُ عَمَلًا وَلَئِن قُلۡتَ إِنَّكُم مَّبۡعُوثُونَ مِنۢ بَعۡدِ ٱلۡمَوۡتِ لَيَقُولَنَّ ٱلَّذِينَ كَفَرُوٓا۟ إِنۡ هَٰذَآ إِلَّا سِحۡرٌ مُّبِينٌ ۝ سورة هود: ٧

He directed His attention to the heaven when it was smoke and fashioned it into seven heavens in two days. He caused each heaven to conform to His orders for it, adorned the lower heaven with lamps, and preserved it from intruders.

It is now known that space is not as empty as once believed. Astronomical observations have detected, both in interstellar space and in nebulae, rarefied matter consisting of about 99 percent gas (mostly hydrogen and helium) and 1 percent dust, i.e., smoke. These dust-size particles have compositions similar to those of such terrestrial materials as silicon compounds, iron oxide, ice crystals, and a host of other small molecules, including organic ones. The original cloud would have consisted mainly of the most common element in the universe: hydrogen. Hydrogen atoms are fast-moving, and only the gravitational pull of a large mass can prevent them from escaping into space. The gasses and dust (smoke) found in the universe might be the remaining residue from the creation of heaven.

Moreover, He directed His attention to the sky, which had been made of smoke. He said to it and to the earth, "Come together, either willingly or not." They replied, "We come together willingly." He then fashioned them into seven firmaments in two days and assigned to each heaven its duty and command. We adorned the lower heaven with lights and with a guard. So decrees God, the One Exalted in Might, Full of Knowledge. (41: 11-12)

ثُمَّ ٱسْتَوَىٰٓ إِلَى ٱلسَّمَآءِ وَهِىَ دُخَانٌ فَقَالَ لَهَا وَلِلْأَرْضِ ٱئْتِيَا طَوْعًا أَوْ كَرْهًا قَالَتَآ أَتَيْنَا طَآئِعِينَ ۝ فَقَضَىٰهُنَّ سَبْعَ سَمَٰوَاتٍ فِى يَوْمَيْنِ وَأَوْحَىٰ فِى كُلِّ سَمَآءٍ أَمْرَهَا وَزَيَّنَّا ٱلسَّمَآءَ ٱلدُّنْيَا بِمَصَٰبِيحَ وَحِفْظًا ذَٰلِكَ تَقْدِيرُ ٱلْعَزِيزِ ٱلْعَلِيمِ ۝

سورة فصلت: ١١-١٢

He created the seven heavens one upon another with no obvious fissures or cracks. The more one looks at them, the more one becomes dazzled and amazed at their making.

He Who created the seven heavens one above the other. You will see no defect of proportion in the creation of God, the Most Gracious. Look again,

ٱلَّذِى خَلَقَ سَبْعَ سَمَٰوَاتٍ طِبَاقًا مَّا تَرَىٰ فِى خَلْقِ ٱلرَّحْمَٰنِ مِن تَفَٰوُتٍ فَٱرْجِعِ ٱلْبَصَرَ هَلْ تَرَىٰ مِن فُطُورٍ ۝

do you see any flaw? Look a second time. What you see will appear to you as dull and discomfited, worn out. (67:3-4)

ثُمَّ ٱرْجِعِ ٱلْبَصَرَ كَرَّتَيْنِ يَنقَلِبْ إِلَيْكَ ٱلْبَصَرُ خَاسِئًا وَهُوَ حَسِيرٌ ۝

سورة الملك: ٣-٤

The heavens and the earth were a "sewn up" mass that God "unstitched." As mentioned above, the heavens were made from smoke. Contemporary scientists support the view that the solar system was formed from a vast cloud of whirling gas and dust that was drifting through space about 5 billion years ago. About 4.6 billion years ago, particles were condensed or drawn together to form a large, dense central mass: the sun. The remaining material, now rotating around the sun, condensed to form planets and other heavenly bodies and were bound to the sun by the force of gravity. This supports what is stated in the Qur'an.

Do the unbelievers not see that the heavens and the earth were joined together (as one unit of creation) before we caused them to separate? We made every living thing from water. Will they still not believe? (21:30)

أَوَلَمْ يَرَ ٱلَّذِينَ كَفَرُوٓاْ أَنَّ ٱلسَّمَٰوَٰتِ وَٱلْأَرْضَ كَانَتَا رَتْقًا فَفَتَقْنَٰهُمَا وَجَعَلْنَا مِنَ ٱلْمَآءِ كُلَّ شَىْءٍ حَىٍّ أَفَلَا يُؤْمِنُونَ ۝

سورة الأنبياء: ٣٠

He raised the heavens without pillars that man can see.

God raised the heavens without any pillars that you can see. Then He established Himself on the Throne (of authority). He subjected the sun and the moon (to His law), and each one runs (its course) for an appointed term. He regulates everything and explains signs in detail so that you may believe with certainty in your meeting with Him. (13:2)

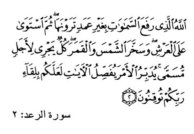

ٱللَّهُ ٱلَّذِى رَفَعَ ٱلسَّمَٰوَٰتِ بِغَيْرِ عَمَدٍ تَرَوْنَهَا ثُمَّ ٱسْتَوَىٰ عَلَى ٱلْعَرْشِ وَسَخَّرَ ٱلشَّمْسَ وَٱلْقَمَرَ كُلٌّ يَجْرِى لِأَجَلٍ مُّسَمًّى يُدَبِّرُ ٱلْأَمْرَ يُفَصِّلُ ٱلْآيَٰتِ لَعَلَّكُم بِلِقَآءِ رَبِّكُمْ تُوقِنُونَ ۝

سورة الرعد: ٢

God has stated that the heavens and the earth possess *aqṭār,* an Arabic word signifying "region" or "diameters." If it is taken to mean diameters, the heavens and the earth would be either oval or round in shape, for these are the only geometrical figures that have diameters. God's throne, His symbol of power and authority, extends over the heavens and the earth.

O Jinn and Men. If you can pass beyond the diameters of the heavens and the earth, then pass. But, you shall not be able to pass without authority. (55:33)

بَـٰمَعْشَرَ ٱلْجِنِّ وَٱلْإِنسِ إِنِ ٱسْتَطَعْتُمْ أَن تَنفُذُواْ مِنْ أَقْطَارِ ٱلسَّمَـٰوَٰتِ وَٱلْأَرْضِ فَٱنفُذُواْ لَا تَنفُذُونَ إِلَّا بِسُلْطَٰنٍ ۝

سورة الرحمن: ٣٣

God! There is no God but He, the Living, the Self-subsisting, the Eternal. Neither slumber nor sleep can seize Him. All things on heaven and earth belong to Him. Who can intercede with Him except those whom He allows to do so? He knows what (appears to His creations as) before, after, or behind them. They shall only gain knowledge of what He wills for them. His Throne extends over the heavens and the earth, and He feels no fatigue while guarding and preserving them, for He is the Most High, the Supreme (in glory). (2:255)

ٱللَّهُ لَا إِلَـٰهَ إِلَّا هُوَ ٱلْحَىُّ ٱلْقَيُّومُ لَا تَأْخُذُهُۥ سِنَةٌ وَلَا نَوْمٌ لَّهُۥ مَا فِى ٱلسَّمَـٰوَٰتِ وَمَا فِى ٱلْأَرْضِ مَن ذَا ٱلَّذِى يَشْفَعُ عِندَهُۥٓ إِلَّا بِإِذْنِهِۦ يَعْلَمُ مَا بَيْنَ أَيْدِيهِمْ وَمَا خَلْفَهُمْ وَلَا يُحِيطُونَ بِشَىْءٍ مِّنْ عِلْمِهِۦٓ إِلَّا بِمَا شَآءَ وَسِعَ كُرْسِيُّهُ ٱلسَّمَـٰوَٰتِ وَٱلْأَرْضَ وَلَا يَـُٔودُهُۥ حِفْظُهُمَا وَهُوَ ٱلْعَلِىُّ ٱلْعَظِيمُ ۝

سورة البقرة: ٢٥٥

Contemporary scientists believe that the universe is probably boundless. Our sun and its planets revolve, along with 100 billion other stars, in the Milky Way galaxy, which is only one galaxy among countless others.

The preceding verses suggest that we live in a universe that is probably round or oval in shape and surrounded by several concentrically arranged heavens. The lowest heaven, which surrounds the inner ball or oval, contains our stars and galaxies. God's throne, which extends over the heavens and Earth, was "on the water" (11:7). The scientific implication of this verse tempted the author to choose its meaning as the title of the book. However, it is very difficult to imagine that the universe is surrounded by water in its liquid state.

Modern science has uncovered two new facts that may shed some light on why God's throne is said to be "on the water." First, space is not empty as one thought, for astronomical observations have detected, both in interstellar space and in nebulae, rarefied matter consisting of about 99 percent gas (mostly hydrogen and helium) and 1 percent dust-size particles having compositions similar to silicon compounds, iron oxide, ice crystals, and a host of other small molecules, including organic ones. Second, scientists now know that, based on quantum mechanics, space is filled with virtual particles and anti-particles that materialize continuously in pairs, separate, and come together repeatedly until they eventually annihilate each other. In other words, they form a "sea" of particles and anti-particles that fill the space of the universe. These could be either electrons and anti-electrons (positrons) or protons and anti-protons.

Contemporary physicists describe atoms as containing only three particles: protons and neutrons, which are located inside the nucleus, and electrons, which are located outside the nucleus. Scientists have been able to build "artificial atoms" with proton and neutron numbers different from those that occur naturally. Such unstable atoms are said to be radioactive. However, these same scientists cannot change one atom into another. For example, the difference between gold (atomic number 79) and iron (atomic number 26) is 53, yet scientists cannot change iron into gold. Such a task is quite easy for God, who is also able to build all atoms of each and every element from the basic particles known to physics, namely, protons, neutrons, and electrons.

Hydrogen, the most common element in space, has been discovered in interstellar space and nebulae. Its atomic number is 1, and its electronic structure is 1s1. Out of this basic element, and with an abundance of particles and anti-particles in the universe, God can create easily all elements by means of nucleosynthesis in the stars. The electronic structure of oxygen is 1s2, 2s2, 2p4, and its atomic number is 8 (fig. 4). So He can easily structure H_2O (water) from hydrogen. This may explain the verse: "His throne was on the water."

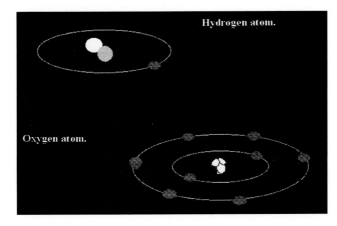

Figure 4: *The atomic structure of hydrogen and oxygen.*

Stars, like the sun, act as huge furnaces in which continuous nuclear reactions occur. Proton–proton reactions are produced when they collide into each other (the proton is the nucleus of a hydrogen atom). Colliding protons build up a nucleus of "heavy hydrogen" and throw off a positron and a neutrino. The "heavy hydrogen" nucleus then combines with another proton to produce "light helium" and a gamma ray, which is the burst of energy that eventually makes its way to the sun's surface. Finally, two "light helium" nuclei fuse and produce an ordinary helium nucleus. This process frees two protons. Nuclear reactions in the sun occur around the core, where the helium remains after its conversion from hydrogen. The resulting energy then rises to the surface and is radiated into space. It is quite possible that, given the size of the "furnaces," all atoms of different elements are baked and produced from the basic and most prevalent atom: hydrogen. Figure 5 attempts to capture all suggestions made about the universe in one illustration. Only God knows what the real structure of the universe looks like.

A ball-shaped universe does not contradict the Big Bang theory, for it has the necessary feature of a point of singularity at the center. Virtual particles and anti-particles have existed in the universe. The presence of such particles in space may be the storehouses where God keeps various elements of matter.

And there is nothing but its (sources) and (inexhaustible) treasures are with Us, but We only send down (what is necessary) in due and ascertainable measure. (15:21)	وَإِن مِّن شَىْءٍ إِلَّا عِندَنَا خَزَآئِنُهُۥ وَمَا نُنَزِّلُهُۥ إِلَّا بِقَدَرٍ مَّعْلُومٍ ۝ سورة الحجر: ٢١

The Qur'an presents strong evidence that the universe is expanding, for God has stated that He created the heavens and is widening them. We know that the universe is expanding at a rate of 5-10 percent every 1 billion years.

We constructed the heavens (universe) with power and skill, for it is We Who steadily expand it. (51:47)	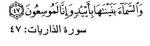 وَٱلسَّمَآءَ بَنَيْنَٰهَا بِأَيْيْدٍ وَإِنَّا لَمُوسِعُونَ ۝ سورة الذاريات: ٤٧

Such a laborious work accomplished by God in His magnificent creation did not leave Him tired or fatigued (50:38). Indeed, one would expect God to be even busier while running the universe's affairs (10:3; 55:29).

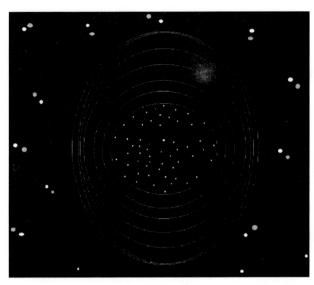

Figure 5: *The universe as suggested by the Qur'an. It has the form of an expanding oval or ball and is made of concentric skies, the nearest of which contains the universe seen from Earth (i.e., the stars and the earth). The world is surrounded by virtual particles and anti-particles as degradation and stores of all atoms, including water molecules.*

We created the heavens and the earth and all that is between them in six days. No sense of weariness touched Us. (50:38)

وَلَقَدْ خَلَقْنَا ٱلسَّمَٰوَٰتِ وَٱلْأَرْضَ وَمَا بَيْنَهُمَا فِى سِتَّةِ أَيَّامٍ وَمَا مَسَّنَا مِن لُّغُوبٍ ﴿٣٨﴾

سورة ق : ٣٨

Truly your Lord is God, Who created the heavens and the earth in six days. Then He established himself on the Throne (of authority), regulating and governing everything. No intercessor (can plead with Him) unless He allows it. This is God your Lord. Therefore, serve (Him). Will you not then keep him in mind? (10:3)

إِنَّ رَبَّكُمُ ٱللَّهُ ٱلَّذِى خَلَقَ ٱلسَّمَٰوَٰتِ وَٱلْأَرْضَ فِى سِتَّةِ أَيَّامٍ ثُمَّ ٱسْتَوَىٰ عَلَى ٱلْعَرْشِ يُدَبِّرُ ٱلْأَمْرَ مَا مِن شَفِيعٍ إِلَّا مِنۢ بَعْدِ إِذْنِهِ ذَٰلِكُمُ ٱللَّهُ رَبُّكُمْ فَٱعْبُدُوهُ أَفَلَا تَذَكَّرُونَ ﴿٣﴾

سورة يونس : ٣

Each creature in the heavens and on the earth asks of Him. Every day He manifests Himself in yet another (wonderous) way. (55:29)

يَسْـَٔلُهُ مَن فِى ٱلسَّمَٰوَٰتِ وَٱلْأَرْضِ كُلَّ يَوْمٍ هُوَ فِى شَأْنٍ ﴿٢٩﴾

سورة الرحمن : ٢٩

This certainly implies that God has no need for rest, as do human beings, and that He is living, everlasting, and has no need for either slumber or sleep (2:255). Although He said that He established Himself upon

the throne after creation, this does not mean that He required rest. If anything, it illustrates His might and ownership of the universe.

God created the heavens and the earth in six days. He is firmly established on the Throne (of authority). He knows what enters the earth and what comes forth from it, what comes down from heaven and what ascends to it. He is with you wherever you are and sees all that you do. (57:4)

هُوَ ٱلَّذِى خَلَقَ ٱلسَّمَوَٰتِ وَٱلْأَرْضَ فِى سِتَّةِ أَيَّامٍ
ثُمَّ ٱسْتَوَىٰ عَلَى ٱلْعَرْشِ يَعْلَمُ مَا يَلِجُ فِى ٱلْأَرْضِ
وَمَا يَخْرُجُ مِنْهَا وَمَا يَنزِلُ مِنَ ٱلسَّمَآءِ وَمَا يَعْرُجُ فِيهَا
وَهُوَ مَعَكُمْ أَيْنَ مَا كُنتُمْ وَٱللَّهُ بِمَا تَعْمَلُونَ بَصِيرٌ ﴿٤﴾

سورة الحديد: ٤

The creation of the heavens and the earth was completed by the sixth
day. Earlier, it was shown that time varies depending upon the object's
location in the universe: one day can be either one thousand or fifty thousand years. The length of the days on our solar system's planets also differ;
it can be as short as eleven hours (Uranus) or as long as 243 days (Venus).
Thus, it is impossible to determine how long a day with God would be,
although science has estimated the approximate duration of various stages
of creation in human terms. God is the light of the heavens and the earth.

God is the light of the heavens and the earth. The parable of His light is thus: there is a niche, and within it a lamp, the lamp enclosed in glass, the glass a brilliant star lit from a blessed tree—an olive tree— neither of the East nor the West, whose oil is luminous, though fire hardly touched it. Light upon light. God guides whom He will to His light. He sets forth parables for men, and He knows all things. (24:35)

ٱللَّهُ نُورُ ٱلسَّمَوَٰتِ وَٱلْأَرْضِ مَثَلُ نُورِهِ
كَمِشْكَوٰةٍ فِيهَا مِصْبَاحٌ ٱلْمِصْبَاحُ فِى زُجَاجَةٍ
ٱلزُّجَاجَةُ كَأَنَّهَا كَوْكَبٌ دُرِّىٌّ يُوقَدُ مِن شَجَرَةٍ
مُّبَٰرَكَةٍ زَيْتُونَةٍ لَّا شَرْقِيَّةٍ وَلَا غَرْبِيَّةٍ يَكَادُ زَيْتُهَا
يُضِىٓءُ وَلَوْ لَمْ تَمْسَسْهُ نَارٌ نُّورٌ عَلَىٰ نُورٍ يَهْدِى
ٱللَّهُ لِنُورِهِ مَن يَشَآءُ وَيَضْرِبُ ٱللَّهُ ٱلْأَمْثَٰلَ
لِلنَّاسِ وَٱللَّهُ بِكُلِّ شَىْءٍ عَلِيمٌ ﴿٣٥﴾

سورة النور: ٣٥

His light is everlasting, and wherever there is light there is day. As
God's light is everlasting, His day must be everlasting. In other words, one
will never know how long it took God to create the universe.

If God opened a gate in heaven and invited man inside to wander
around, he would be dazzled and believe himself bewitched.

Even if We opened to them a
gate of heaven and they ascend-
ed therein all day, they would
say, "Our eyes have been intox-
icated. We have been bewitched
by sorcery." (15:14-15)

وَلَوْ فَتَحْنَا عَلَيْهِم بَابًا مِّنَ ٱلسَّمَاءِ فَظَلُّوا فِيهِ
يَعْرُجُونَ ۝ لَقَالُوٓا إِنَّمَا سُكِّرَتْ أَبْصَارُنَا
بَلْ نَحْنُ قَوْمٌ مَّسْحُورُونَ ۝

سورة الحجر: ١٤-١٥

He prevents the heavens from falling on our planet (22:65), has provided them with a well-guarded canopy (21:32), and has filled them with
numerous paths representing the orbits of planets around each star (51:7).

Do you not see that God has
made everything on earth subject to you, and the ships that
sail on the seas by His command? He does not allow the
sky (rain) to fall on the earth
except by His will, for He is
Most Kind and Most Merciful
to man. (22:65)

أَلَمْ تَرَ أَنَّ ٱللَّهَ سَخَّرَ لَكُم مَّا فِي ٱلْأَرْضِ وَٱلْفُلْكَ تَجْرِى
فِي ٱلْبَحْرِ بِأَمْرِهِ وَيُمْسِكُ ٱلسَّمَاءَ أَن تَقَعَ
عَلَى ٱلْأَرْضِ إِلَّا بِإِذْنِهِ إِنَّ ٱللَّهَ بِٱلنَّاسِ
لَرَءُوفٌ رَّحِيمٌ ۝

سورة الحج: ٥٦

We have made the heavens as
a well-guarded canopy, but
still they turn away from the
signs that these things (point
to)! (21:32)

وَجَعَلْنَا ٱلسَّمَاءَ سَقْفًا مَّحْفُوظًا
وَهُمْ عَنْ ءَايَٰتِهَا مُعْرِضُونَ ۝

سورة الأنبياء: ٣٢

By the sky with (its) numerous
paths. (51:7)

وَٱلسَّمَاءِ ذَاتِ ٱلْحُبُكِ ۝

سورة الذاريات: ٧

All inhabitants of Earth, whether organic or inorganic, require the lowest heaven (i.e., stars, clouds, and rain) for their very existence. It is the only
part of heaven that is visible to all forms of life on Earth's surface. For this
reason, God created the lowest heaven in such a way that it would protect
Earth's organic and inorganic inhabitants from destruction or decay. He
created the stars as adornments in the lower heaven (37:6) and arranged
them in constellations (25:61). Thus, it is not surprising that God should use
the position of stars as a mighty oath (56:75-76).

We have indeed adorned the
skies nearest to the earth with
the beauty of stars—(37:6)

إِنَّا زَيَّنَّا ٱلسَّمَاءَ ٱلدُّنْيَا بِزِينَةٍ ٱلْكَوَاكِبِ ۝

سورة الصافات: ٦

Blessed is He Who made constellations in the skies, and

تَبَارَكَ ٱلَّذِى جَعَلَ فِي ٱلسَّمَاءِ بُرُوجًا وَجَعَلَ فِيهَا

placed therein a lamp and a light-giving moon. (25:61)

سُرَجًا وَقَمَرًا مُّنِيرًا ۝

سورة الفرقان: ٦١

Furthermore, I call the setting of the stars to witness, and that is indeed a mighty adjuration, if you but knew—(56:75-76)

فَلَا أُقْسِمُ بِمَوَٰقِعِ ٱلنُّجُومِ ۝

وَإِنَّهُ لَقَسَمٌ لَّوْ تَعْلَمُونَ عَظِيمٌ ۝

سورة الواقعة: ٧٥-٧٦

In 150 AC, the Greek astronomer Ptolemy listed 48 constellations. A total of 88 constellations are now known to cover the northern and southern skies. As stated earlier, countless stars are strung out in space, but only about two thousand are visible to the naked eye at any one time from Earth.

Stars were also created to "protect (the heavens) against rebel satans" (37:7). They tried to touch heaven to listen to the high council (37:8) but found that the lowest heaven was full of "tracking piercing flames" that attacked them from every side (37:6-10; 72:8-9).

We have adorned the skies nearest to the earth with stars (for beauty) and to guard against all obstinate rebellious evil spirits, (so) that they should not be able to listen to the Exalted Assembly but be cast away from every side, repulsed, for they are under a perpetual penalty, except those who snatch something by stealth. They are pursued by a flaming fire of piercing brightness. (37:6-10)

إِنَّا زَيَّنَّا ٱلسَّمَآءَ ٱلدُّنْيَا بِزِينَةٍ ٱلْكَوَاكِبِ ۝

وَحِفْظًا مِّن كُلِّ شَيْطَٰنٍ مَّارِدٍ ۝

لَّا يَسَّمَّعُونَ إِلَى ٱلْمَلَإِ ٱلْأَعْلَىٰ وَيُقْذَفُونَ مِن كُلِّ جَانِبٍ ۝

دُحُورًا وَلَهُمْ عَذَابٌ وَاصِبٌ ۝

إِلَّا مَنْ خَطِفَ ٱلْخَطْفَةَ فَأَتْبَعَهُ شِهَابٌ ثَاقِبٌ ۝

سورة الصافات: ٨-١٠

And we reached out towards heaven, but we found it filled with stern guards and flaming fires. Indeed, we used to sit there in (hidden) stations to hear (what was being said), but any one who listens now will find a flaming fire waiting for him in ambush. (72:8-9)

وَأَنَّا لَمَسْنَا ٱلسَّمَآءَ فَوَجَدْنَٰهَا مُلِئَتْ حَرَسًا شَدِيدًا وَشُهُبًا ۝

وَأَنَّا كُنَّا نَقْعُدُ مِنْهَا مَقَٰعِدَ لِلسَّمْعِ فَمَن يَسْتَمِعِ ٱلْآنَ يَجِدْ لَهُ شِهَابًا رَّصَدًا ۝

سورة الجن: ٨-٩

It is very interesting that the word *raṣad* is used to describe the type of piercing flame awaiting the intruders. In Arabic, this word signifies a three-dimensional point in space at a specific point of time and often is used to indicate the position of celestial bodies. Given this, *raṣad* describes how the piercing flame reaches an intruder by anticipating its three-dimensional trajectory in a specified fraction of time. This is not unlike modern rockets.

God created a lamp (the sun) and the light-giving moon (25:61). He left no doubt about the nature of both objects.

Blessed is He Who made constellations in the skies and placed therein a (radiant) lamp and a light-giving moon. (25:61)	تَبَارَكَ ٱلَّذِى جَعَلَ فِى ٱلسَّمَآءِ بُرُوجًا وَجَعَلَ فِيهَا سِرَٰجًا وَقَمَرًا مُّنِيرًا ۝ سورة الفرقان: ٦١
Do you not see how God has created the seven heavens, one above another, made the moon a light in their midst, and made the sun as a (radiant) lamp? (71:15-16)	أَلَمْ تَرَوْا۟ كَيْفَ خَلَقَ ٱللَّهُ سَبْعَ سَمَٰوَٰتٍ طِبَاقًا ۝ وَجَعَلَ ٱلْقَمَرَ فِيهِنَّ نُورًا وَجَعَلَ ٱلشَّمْسَ سِرَٰجًا ۝ سورة نوح: ١٦

The sun provides the light and the heat upon which all life on Earth depends. Its light takes 8 minutes and 20 seconds to cross the 93-million-mile gap to us. The sun's size is ideal. If it were as big as the red giant Betelgeux in the constellation of Orion the Hunter, it would engulf Earth. If oue plante orbited the Blue Giant Rigel, all life on it would have roasted. This demonstrates how the sun's mass (333,000 times that of Earth, or 20×10^{30} kg) and temperature has made life possible on Earth. Otherwise, life might have developed on Mars or another planet, according to God's will.

Contemporary scientists say that our sun was formed 4.7 billion years ago. Its surface temperature is roughly 6,000°C, and its center's temperature is estimated to be 15,000,000°C. Under these conditions, atoms are crushed together in nuclear fusion reactions, as if they were in a hydrogen bomb, and generate a glowing brightness that is visible to the human eye. During this process, many hydrogen atoms are transformed into helium atoms. Those that are not are changed into the energy that appears on the sun's surface as light and heat. According to scientists, 4 million tons of hydrogen are turned into energy every second. Based on this formula, it will take at least another 5 billion years for the sun to exhaust its fuel.

Recent scientific progress has made it possible for man to appreciate the fact that the sun will eventually consume its nuclear fuel and die. God has ordained that the sun and the moon run a determined course that will last for as long as He desires (31:29). The sun cannot catch the moon, and each is swimming in a special orbit (36:40).

Do you not see that God merges night into day and day into night, that He has subjected the sun and the moon (to His law), each running its course for a term appointed, and that He is well acquainted with all that you do? (31:29)

أَلَمْ تَرَ أَنَّ ٱللَّهَ يُولِجُ ٱلَّيْلَ فِى ٱلنَّهَارِ وَيُولِجُ ٱلنَّهَارَ
فِى ٱلَّيْلِ وَسَخَّرَ ٱلشَّمْسَ وَٱلْقَمَرَ كُلٌّ يَجْرِى
إِلَىٰٓ أَجَلٍ مُّسَمًّى وَأَنَّ ٱللَّهَ بِمَا تَعْمَلُونَ خَبِيرٌ ۝

سورة لقمان: ٢٩

The sun is not allowed to catch up with the moon, nor the night to outstrip the day. Each swims along in (its own) orbit (according to His law). (36:40)

لَا ٱلشَّمْسُ يَنۢبَغِى لَهَآ أَن تُدْرِكَ ٱلْقَمَرَ وَلَا ٱلَّيْلُ
سَابِقُ ٱلنَّهَارِ وَكُلٌّ فِى فَلَكٍ يَسْبَحُونَ ۝

سورة يس: ٤٠

The Arabic word *sabaḥa* (lit. to swim) is used to describe the movement of the sun and the moon in space. This implies that they actually swim in orbit in some form of medium. There has been a long-standing debate among scientists as to what constitutes the universe's empty space. In the past, it was believed that the universe was filled with virtual particles and anti-particles. Nobody knows whether or not they represent the medium in which the sun and the moon swim according to the the special orbit determined for them by God. The sun, the moon, and the stars are subservient to His command (7:54). In addition, the movement of the first two is not haphazard, as can be proven by mathematical calculations (55:5), and the sun obviously moves to a particular place (36:38). He decreed that the moon would exist in stations or houses until it returns, like an aged palm-bough, to the beginning of its orbit (36:39).

Your Guardian-Lord is God, the Creator of the heavens and the earth in six days, Who then established Himself on the Throne (of authority). He draws the night as a veil over the day, each seeking the other in rapid succession. He created the sun, the moon, and the stars, (all of which) are governed by His law. Is it not His (right) to create and to govern? Blessed be He, the Cherisher and Sustainer of the Worlds! (7:54)

إِنَّ رَبَّكُمُ ٱللَّهُ ٱلَّذِى خَلَقَ ٱلسَّمَـٰوَٰتِ وَٱلْأَرْضَ
فِى سِتَّةِ أَيَّامٍ ثُمَّ ٱسْتَوَىٰ عَلَى ٱلْعَرْشِ يُغْشِى
ٱلَّيْلَ ٱلنَّهَارَ يَطْلُبُهُۥ حَثِيثًا وَٱلشَّمْسَ وَٱلْقَمَرَ
وَٱلنُّجُومَ مُسَخَّرَٰتٍۭ بِأَمْرِهِۦٓ أَلَا لَهُ ٱلْخَلْقُ
وَٱلْأَمْرُ تَبَارَكَ ٱللَّهُ رَبُّ ٱلْعَـٰلَمِينَ ۝

سورة الأعراف: ٥٤

The sun and the moon follow courses that have been determined (exactly). (55:5)

ٱلشَّمْسُ وَٱلْقَمَرُ بِحُسْبَانٍ ﴿٥﴾

سورة الرحمن: ٥

The sun runs its course for the time that has been determined for it. That is the decree of (God), the Exalted in Might, the All-Knowing. In addition, We have measured mansions for the moon (to traverse) until it returns like the old (and withered) lower part of a date stalk. (36:38-39)

وَٱلشَّمْسُ تَجْرِى لِمُسْتَقَرٍّ لَّهَا ذَٰلِكَ تَقْدِيرُ ٱلْعَزِيزِ ٱلْعَلِيمِ ﴿٣٨﴾ وَٱلْقَمَرَ قَدَّرْنَٰهُ مَنَازِلَ حَتَّىٰ عَادَ كَٱلْعُرْجُونِ ٱلْقَدِيمِ ﴿٣٩﴾

سورة يس: ٣٨-٣٩

The moon's diameter is approximately one quarter that of Earth. It has no atmosphere or water and simply rotates around Earth. Man first landed on it during July 1969 and found no evidence of either past or present life. It will be shown in chapter seven that the moon is the basis for celestial navigation and calendars.

Without the creation of the lowest heaven, which contains the sun, the moon, the stars, and the clouds, no life could exist on Earth. The heavens contain several tracts and paths (23:17; 51:7), and the lowest heaven is protected from the jinn (invisible creatures) by rocket-like stars. In many science fiction films, people try to reach the higher heavens via space ships. They presume that the gates to these higher heavens are through black holes. However, they later realize that these are traps from which no man or object can return. It is easy to speculate on the lower heaven, but difficult to speculate on those that are remote.

We have made seven tracts above you and are never unmindful of (Our) creation. (23:17)

وَلَقَدْ خَلَقْنَا فَوْقَكُمْ سَبْعَ طَرَآئِقَ وَمَا كُنَّا عَنِ ٱلْخَلْقِ غَٰفِلِينَ ﴿١٧﴾

سورة المؤمنون: ١٧

By the sky, with its numerous paths. (51:7)

وَٱلسَّمَآءِ ذَاتِ ٱلْحُبُكِ ﴿٧﴾

سورة الذاريات: ٧

And He is in the highest part of the horizon. (53:7)

وَهُوَ بِٱلْأُفُقِ ٱلْأَعْلَىٰ ﴿٧﴾

سورة النجم: ٧

CHAPTER THREE

THE CREATION OF EARTH

Modern Scientific Knowledge

Industrialization and modernization have caused severe damage to our environment as well as great anxiety and concern among people. Heads of state meet regularly to discuss environmental problems, especially global warming. Everybody is trying to make Earth a better place in which to live, and hopefully man will leave it to his children in a better condition.

If Earth is compared to other planets in the solar system, it can be described quite simply as being custom-made for human beings and for over a million other life forms. Its average temperature is 22°C, whereas those of Mercury and Pluto are 520°C and -230°C, respectively. Our planet is surrounded by the right mixture of gasses, among them the one on which all of its forms of life depend: oxygen. Earth's gravity is just enough to keep its surrounding gasses from escaping into space.

Origin of the Planet Earth

At one time, scientists thought Earth was created by the collision of giant tongues of material torn from the pre-existing sun by the gravitational attraction of a passing star. This material then flew toward the sun and circled it as cold bodies. This hypothesis, however, is quite weak, for material torn from the sun would be very hot (about 1,000,000°C) and would be in the form of gas that would disperse into space. A second theory suggests that the sun, at some stage, was growing rapidly in size and rotating at a high speed. It eventually ejected a stream of gas and dust that then formed a spinning disc around it. At a later date, the planets were formed from this material. Most scientists now accept a third theory, which is based on the discovery that space is not as empty as once thought and that it contains rarefied matter consisting of about 99 percent gas and

1 percent dust in interstellar space and nebulae. Scientists considered the possibility that the solar system was formed from a vast cloud of whirling gas and dust that was drifting through space about 5 billion years ago. About 4.6 billion years ago, particles condensed or were drawn together to form a large dense central mass: The sun. The remaining material, still rotating around the sun, condensed to form the planets and other heavenly bodies bound to the sun by the force of gravity.

Geological Background

In 1785, James Hutton of Edinburgh became the first individual to describe the cycle of erosion and uplift. He presented Earth as a giant machine that is in constant motion. According to him, the continents are undergoing constant and gradual erosion. The debris that results from this process is washed down to the sea, accumulates as sediment, is compacted through the effect of the planet's heat, and is then uplifted and contorted. Earth's heat, which is sufficient to melt rocks at great depths, then causes this melted material to move into the upper crust and be subjected to erosion. Hutton was denounced as an atheist for his theory.

Geology became an important subject during the nineteenth century. Geologists, using fossils and the law of "super-position" (e.g., the upper strata is usually younger than the lower) to arrange rocks according to their age, produced great numbers of geological maps. The subject became the key to the industrial revolution, for it allowed experts to recognize the presence of raw materials and to identify the best places for canals, roads, railways, and other items necessary for a suitable infrastructure.

The second revolution did not start until after the 1960s, when the new science of plate tectonics came into its own. This science held that the continents, which until then had been considered stationary, were actually drifting. Ocean floors, believed to be old and inactive, were found to be young and in motion. Earth's outer shell, thought to be in one part or perhaps two (e.g., oceanic and continental), was found to be divided into 15 plates that reacted with their neighbors along their edges.

Continental Drift

The continental drift theory and the birth of the "super-continent" of Alfred Wegener, son of a evangelical preacher in Berlin, was published during 1912-24. He named this supercontinent *Pangea* (fig. 6) and claimed that, at an unknown date in the past, it had fragmented into sev-

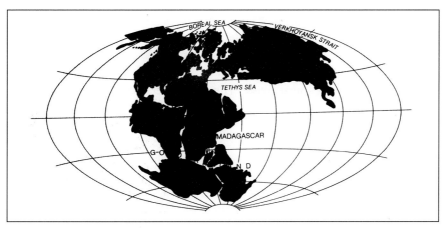

Figure 6: *A diagram of the super-continent Pangea (according to J. Tuzo Wilson, Continental Drift (Scientific America:1963).*

eral continents. Each of these new continents then drifted slowly to its present position. His theory did not find much support, even after Alexander du Toit's book *Our Wandering Continents* (1937) provided new data supporting his hypothesis. The earth sciences, which began in the late 1950s, also provided supporting evidence. For example, the study of fossils provided paleontological evidence for the theory of continental drift: glossopteris fern seed was found on all five continents, special reptiles found in Africa were found in South America, and such geological correlations as rock formations and structural features were shown to be similar across continental edges. The supercontinent Pangea was surrounded by the universal ocean *Panthalassa.*

The first split caused *Laurasia* to move to the north and eventually gave rise to North America, Europe, and most of Asia. To the south, *Gondwana* gave rise to South America, Africa, Australia, Antarctica, and India. During the last 200 million years, they began to separate and form the continents that we see today. About 135 million years ago, India began an unusually rapid northward journey toward Asia, with which it was to collide and unite about 30 million years ago. The rate of continental drift is usually considered to be in the range of 0-7 centimeters per year.

Plate Tectonics

Irrefutable evidence of continental drift came from advances in the field of paleomagnetism during the late 1950s and early 1960s. It is now more than just matching the continental edges on a map, for earth scientists can measure the level of magnetization locked in rocks. When a rock is formed, its magnetic particles are aligned along Earth's magnetic field. Once the orientation of a rock's magnetic particles is measured via trigonometry, the latitude at which the rock was formed and the past orientation of the continent upon which it lay can be determined. In addition, these readings can give the position of the north magnetic pole at that particular time.

This is how global paleomagnetic data maps were plotted for ancient positions of the north pole. When this study was performed, experts found that earlier north poles lay along a smooth curve, termed a "polar wander curve," that led away from the present pole. There were only two explanations: either the magnetic pole had moved gradually to its present position or the continents had moved. When this procedure was applied to other continents, the polar wander curves did not coincide. As there can only be one north magnetic pole at a time, the diversion curves must indicate that the continents had moved with respect to one another in the past.

Different continents have different polar wander curves, a phenomenon that indicates movement in different directions relative to the pole and to one another. Australia can be shown to have moved from the region of the south pole to its present position during the last 200 million years. The supercontinent Pangea seems to have existed until about 200 million years ago. When it fragmented into smaller landmasses, it did so along a series of cracks or faults at various weak points. The land bounded by the faults subsided and formed a rift valley. The great rift valley of East Africa, which stretches from East Africa through the Red Sea and ends in the vicinity of the Jordan Valley, shows that continental drift still continues at the rate of a few centimeters a year. It is postulated that, in 50 million years, this valley might widen into a structure like the Red Sea, East Africa will break away, and Africa will become a separate continent.

Another magnetic message was found while studying oceanic ridges (fig. 7). Although rocks become magnetized parallel to the local direction of Earth's magnetic field at the time of their formation, only 50 percent of them are magnetized in the same direction as the magnetic field. The other 50 percent are magnetized in precisely the opposite direction. As a result, they are classified as "normal" and "reverse" magnetized rocks, respectively. It was later concluded that "reverse" magnetized rocks were

Figure 7: Oceanic ridges show-ing where the earth plates (lithosphere) meet.

formed while Earth's magnetic field itself must have been reversed. In such a situation, a compass needle would point to the south rather than to the north.

The magnetic field is switching continually from one polarity to the other. Molten mantles rise at the oceanic ridge and form an oceanic lithos-phere. This mass then cools, solidifies, and becomes magnetized in the plante's field direction. Later, it spreads on either side of the ridge in order to make way for a new mantle. The next wave will be magnetized in the direction of the current magnetic field, which could be in the reverse direc-tion. Alternations in the magnetic field are recorded on the ocean floor, which acts as a record of Earth's millions of years of history.

Magnetized rock on the ocean floor will reveal its own magnetic effect on Earth's surface. Sensitive instruments towed behind a survey ship can detect both normal and reversed magnetic fields and plot the position of magnetized rocks. The interpretation of these magnetic observations was reported in 1963 by two British geophysicists, Fred Vine and Drummond Matthews, who presented the oceanic ridge's zebra-stripe pattern as evi-dence of a spreading sea floor and a reversal of Earth's magnetic field.

It is not only the continents that move—the ocean floor also moves, for it pushes and carries the continents along. The layer that carries the ocean and the continents is known as the lithosphere. Huge mountain ranges exist through all of the major oceans. They are almost linked, are about 80,000 kms. long, and are about 3 kms. in height above the adjacent ocean basin. These mountain ranges are referred to as oceanic ridges. Along a narrow band of their axis, molten material from the asthenosphere, located under the lithosphere, eventually rises up at the oceanic ridge and spreads along either side of it (fig. 7). The process then continues as explained before. Thus, the ocean floor is in a process of continual change and expansion.

A lithosphere's destruction occurs along narrow regions known as subduction zones. At such a point, the spreading lithosphere bends downward at an angle of roughly 45°, reenters Earth's interior, melts slowly, and is reassimilated. As both cannot be reassimilated into the earth when there is a collision between two plates, one tends to override the other. The result is the formation of mountains that serve as wedges to stop further subduction.

According to plate tectonics, there are three main types of plate boundaries: 1) those with oceanic ridges, which are points at which the planet is extending and where a new oceanic lithosphere is created; 2) subduction zones, at which locations portions of the planet are destroyed due to destructive boundaries along the area where an earlier oceanic lithosphere has been consumed; and 3) conservative boundaries, along which a lithosphere is neither created nor destroyed. These are "transform faults," which contain the zigzags along which oceanic ridges are made. At the ridge, two adjacent plates move each other without adding any new material. All three types of plate boundaries generate earthquakes, yet only constructive and destructive boundaries are associated with volcanic activity.

There are 15 major lithospheric plates of various sizes and several minor ones (i.e., microplates). Most plates, which are about 75 kms. thick, carry both the ocean and the continent. Horizontal distortion is much more difficult to achieve than vertical distortion. The asthenosphere's mobility allows the overlying lithosphere plates to move horizontally. The slab-pull force produced by subduction inside the planet, to a depth of approximately 700 kms., is the main force that can cause the lithospheres to move.

Volcanoes erupt when molten rock (magma) moves from Earth's interior toward the surface through a weakness in the lithosphere. This material passes through in two ways: 1) via linear fissures or fractures (81 percent of volcanoes are located on the sea bed or oceanic ridges that cannot be seen) and 2) at particular points (19 percent). Two thirds of these are created along the boundaries of a destructive plate. The remaining third forms central-vent volcanoes, which are commonly referred to as volcanoes. They are located on the ocean floor and cannot be seen. Only 0.6 percent of conventional central-vent volcanoes appear on Earth's surface.

Earthquakes are the result of a sudden release of energy that has accumulated slowly in a local region of Earth's crust or upper mantle. The point where this is created is called the focus or the hypercenter, and the corresponding area on the surface is called the epicenter. The extent of destruction depends on whether or not there is a city in the epicenter's area. Earthquakes derive their destructive power from the motions of lithosphere plates as they interact along their margins. Strain is built up, rocks located at the interface suddenly rupture, and the result is seismic activity or earthquakes. Most earthquakes occur along such plate boundaries as oceanic ridges, subduction zones, and transform faults. However, they may occur in plates located far from the edges that have deeply situated unactivated faults left over from earlier plate tectonic phases.

Earth's interior is inaccessible to man. The deepest mine is less than 4 kms. inside the planet. The Russians had an ambitious drilling program and, in 1984, managed to reach 11 kms. (their desired target was 15 kms.). As Earth's average radius is 6,370 kms., man is only scratching its surface. All studies of the interior must be done by indirect techniques and are mostly dependent on seismic waves, which can identify Earth's layers.

This is the level of knowledge that science has reached so far. It seems that scientists are supporting the Qur'anic statement that the heavens and the earth were originally smoke (41:11-12). As mentioned earlier, it has been discovered that space is not as empty as once thought. Astronomical observations have detected, both in interstellar space and in nebulae, rarefied matter consisting of about 99 percent gas (mostly hydrogen and helium) and 1 percent dust (i.e., smoke) consisting of dust-size particles having a composition similar to such terrestrial materials as silicon compounds, iron oxide, ice crystals, and a host of other small molecules, including organic ones. The original cloud would have consisted mainly of the most abundant element in the universe: hydrogen. Hydrogen atoms are fast-moving, and only the gravitational pull of a large mass can prevent them from escaping into space. In this chapter, a brief collation of the Qur'anic account of Earth's creation is given and existing evidence from scientific facts will be discussed.

Earth's Structure as Suggested by the Qur'an

Shape

It has already been stated that Earth's diameter indicates that it is either oval or ball-shaped. Further evidence is provided when God says that He "enballs" the night over the day and "enballs" the day over the night (fig. 8). This indicates the shape of the planet.

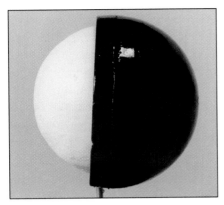 

Figures 8 a & b: *Illustration of the Qur'anic verse in which God says: "He 'enballs' the nigh over the day and He 'enballs' the day over the night." This indicates that the earth is oval or ball-shaped.*

He created the heavens and the earth in true (proportions). He makes the night overlap the day, and the day overlap the night. He has subjected the sun and the moon (to His law). Each one follows a course for an appointed time. Is He not the Exalted in Power, He Who forgives again and again? (39:5)

خَلَقَ ٱلسَّمَٰوَٰتِ وَٱلْأَرْضَ بِٱلْحَقِّ يُكَوِّرُ ٱلَّيْلَ عَلَى ٱلنَّهَارِ وَيُكَوِّرُ ٱلنَّهَارَ عَلَى ٱلَّيْلِ وَسَخَّرَ ٱلشَّمْسَ وَٱلْقَمَرَ كُلٌّ يَجْرِى لِأَجَلٍ مُّسَمًّى أَلَا هُوَ ٱلْعَزِيزُ ٱلْغَفَّٰرُ ۝

سورة الزمر: ٥

Further evidence that the planet is ball-shaped is given when God calls Himself the Lord of the easts and the wests. This fact must have been accepted easily by the people of that time, for they could see its truth by watching the horizon and viewing the sunrise at different points in the east, depending upon the season, in a north-to-south arc. However, as explained earlier, the time of the sun's rising varies by four minutes for each degree of longitude. This is a leading indication that our planet is ball-shaped.

I call to witness (Our being) the Lord of all points in the east and the west that We can certainly ... (70:40)

فَلَا أُقْسِمُ بِرَبِّ ٱلْمَشَٰرِقِ وَٱلْمَغَٰرِبِ إِنَّا لَقَٰدِرُونَ ۝

سورة المعارج: ٤٠

Layers of the Earth

God said that He created seven heavens and a similar number for the planet Earth.

God is the One Who created seven firmaments and a similar number for the earth. His command penetrates (all) of them, that you may know that He has power over everything and that His knowledge surrounds everything. (65:12)

اللَّهُ الَّذِى خَلَقَ سَبْعَ سَمَوَاتٍ وَمِنَ الْأَرْضِ مِثْلَهُنَّ يَتَنَزَّلُ الْأَمْرُ بَيْنَهُنَّ لِتَعْلَمُوا أَنَّ اللَّهَ عَلَى كُلِّ شَىْءٍ قَدِيرٌ وَأَنَّ اللَّهَ قَدْ أَحَاطَ بِكُلِّ شَىْءٍ عِلْمًا ۝

سورة الطلاق: ١٢

This verse could have two interpretations. The first is that He created several planets similar to ours. His statement that He is the "Lord of the worlds" (1:2), an assertion that indicates a multiplicity of worlds either similar or dissimilar to ours supports this. However, the verse asserts their existence and is repeated several times a day as part of the ritual prayer. This is perhaps to remind people of His countless and diverse creations.

All praise is due to God, the Lord of the worlds. (1:1)

الْحَمْدُ لِلَّهِ رَبِّ الْعَالَمِينَ ۝

سورة الفاتحة: ١

An alternative explanation is found in 65:12: God fashioned Earth into layers just as He took heaven, which was one big mass, and fashioned it into layers one upon another. It seems that our planet is unique in God's creation and that other solar systems might not contain an identical planet.

All Qur'anic verses on the universe's creation state that the heavens are plural and Earth is singular. The following verses show how God established the plurality of the heavens and the singularity of our planet.

The unbelievers say, "The Hour will never come to us." Reply, "By my Lord, by the One who knows the unseen, from whom not even the least atom in the heavens or the earth is hidden, it will come to you. Regardless of size, everything is recorded in a clear record. (34:3)

وَقَالَ الَّذِينَ كَفَرُوا لَا تَأْتِينَا السَّاعَةُ قُلْ بَلَى وَرَبِّى لَتَأْتِيَنَّكُمْ عَالِمِ الْغَيْبِ لَا يَعْزُبُ عَنْهُ مِثْقَالُ ذَرَّةٍ فِى السَّمَوَاتِ وَلَا فِى الْأَرْضِ وَلَا أَصْغَرُ مِنْ ذَلِكَ وَلَا أَكْبَرُ إِلَّا فِى كِتَابٍ مُبِينٍ ۝

سورة سبأ: ٣

The seven heavens and the earth, and all beings therein, declare His glory. All things celebrate His praise, and yet you do not understand how they declare His glory. Truly He is Oft-Forbearing, Most Forgiving. (17:44)

تُسَبِّحُ لَهُ السَّمَوَاتُ السَّبْعُ وَالْأَرْضُ وَمَنْ فِيهِنَّ وَإِنْ مِنْ شَىْءٍ إِلَّا يُسَبِّحُ بِحَمْدِهِ وَلَكِنْ لَا تَفْقَهُونَ تَسْبِيحَهُمْ إِنَّهُ كَانَ حَلِيمًا غَفُورًا ۝

سورة الإسراء: ٤٤

A revelation from the Creator of the earth and the heavens on high ... to Him belongs what is in the heavens and on the earth, as well as what is between them and what is beneath the soil. (20:4, 6)

تَنزِيلًا مِّمَّنْ خَلَقَ ٱلْأَرْضَ وَٱلسَّمَـٰوَٰتِ ٱلْعُلَى ۝

لَهُۥ مَا فِى ٱلسَّمَـٰوَٰتِ وَمَا فِى ٱلْأَرْضِ
وَمَا بَيْنَهُمَا وَمَا تَحْتَ ٱلثَّرَىٰ ۝

سورة طه: ٤-٦

Say: "The (Qur'an) was sent down by God, who knows the secret (that is) in the heavens and the earth. Truly, He is Oft-Forgiving, Most Merciful. (25:6)

قُلْ أَنزَلَهُ ٱلَّذِى يَعْلَمُ ٱلسِّرَّ فِى ٱلسَّمَـٰوَٰتِ
وَٱلْأَرْضِ إِنَّهُۥ كَانَ غَفُورًا رَّحِيمًا ۝

سورة الفرقان: ٦

There is now strong scientific evidence that Earth is made of seven layers. Several authors have suggested that, in the beginning, our planet was probably a homogeneous mixture without continents or oceans. In the process of differentiation, iron sank to the center and lighter material floated upward to form a crust. As a result, Earth became a zoned planet with a dense iron core, a superficial crust of light rock, and a residual mantle that functions as a buffer zone. After careful seismic and other studies, it has been suggested that Earth has seven layers (illustrated in fig. 9): 1) a continental crust (0-40 kms.) and an oceanic crust (0-10 kms.), 2) a lithosphere (0-70 kms.), 3) an asthenosphere (70-250 kms.), 4) a transitional zone (250-700 kms.), 5) a lower mantle (700-2,900 kms.), 6) a liquid iron core (2,900-4,980 kms.), and 7) a solid iron core (4,980-6,371 kms.).

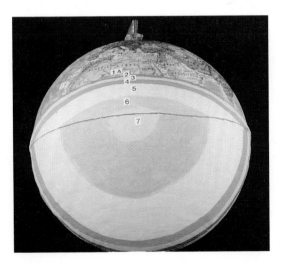

Figure 9: Model showing the seven layers of the Earth: 1a) continental crust and 1b) oceanic crust, 2) lithosphere (rawāsī), 3) asthenosphere, 4) transitional zone, 5) lower mantle, 6) liquid iron core, and 7) solid iron core.

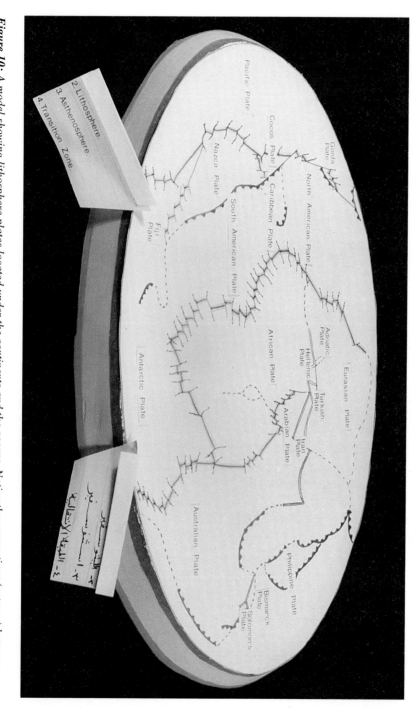

Figure 10: *A model showing lithosphere plates located under the continents and the oceans. Notice the connections (sutures) between them—they resemble a human skull. The plates correspond to the rawāsī of the Qur'an.*

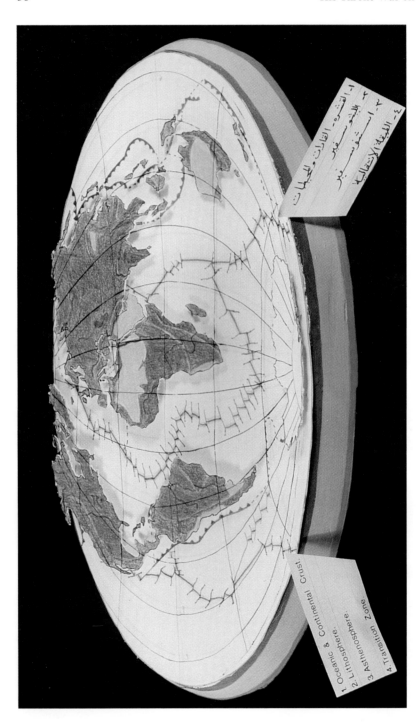

Figure 11: A model showing the plates carrying the continents and the oceans.

Thus it is clear that our planet consists of seven layers, as indicated in the Qur'an. Scientific research tells us the plante's radius is 6,371 kms. and, with a total mass of 6.6 hundred trillion tons, has a density of approximately 16 at the center and of 2.7 at the surface. Seismic records show that shock waves passing through the earth change their direction and speed at certain levels, a phenomenon known as discontinuity. Earth's layers were assumed, and it was recognized later that the continents rest on 15 major plates, which are named for the continent in question (fig. 10).

These plates, known as the lithosphere layer and as bearers of the planet's crust (both continents and oceans), move along Earth's molten core (fig. 11). They are made of solidified rock approximately 70 kms. thick and act as a thermal boundary conduction layer floating on the asthenosphere's molten or semimolten rock. At the interface of two plates, one tends to be pushed downward (subduction zone), which causes that lithosphere plate to descend into the hot molten mantle under the second plate's leading edge. This would have continued, and the plate's continent would have disappeared, if the top of the second plate's leading edge had no mountains. These mountains, trapped between one plate's descending subduction zone and the leading edge of the mountain-bearing second plate, prevent the plate with the continental crust on top from slipping into the interior (fig. 12).

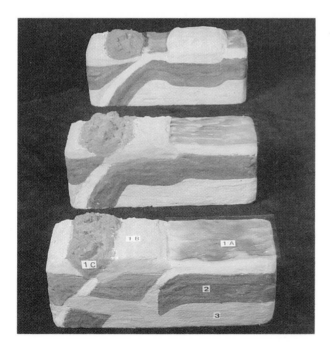

Figure 12: A model illustrating how a lithosphere plate *(rawāsī) (2)* with the oceans *(1A)* and the continents *(1B)* sink into the earth under the leading edge of another plate (see upper and middle models). The lower model shows how the mountain range *(1C),* acting as a wedge between the plates, prevents the continent-bearing lithosphere from sinking into the earth.

Recent findings and theories throw light on the Qur'anic statement that our planet has seven layers. God also said that the time He took to create Earth was similar to the time that it He took to create the universe. Thus although the planet is small, its creation must have been on a vast scale.

Say: "Do you deny Him who created the earth in two days, and do you join others with Him as equal? He is the Lord of (all) the worlds." (41:9)

قُلْ أَئِنَّكُمْ لَتَكْفُرُونَ بِالَّذِى خَلَقَ ٱلْأَرْضَ فِى يَوْمَيْنِ وَتَجْعَلُونَ لَهُۥٓ أَندَادًا ذَٰلِكَ رَبُّ ٱلْعَٰلَمِينَ ٩

سورة فصلت: ٩

He also said that He set *rawāsī* on top of it.

He placed on the (earth) *ra-wāsī* that stand firm and high above it. He blessed the earth and measured all things therein so that they would receive their nourishment in due proportion, in four days, according to (the needs of) those who seek (sustenance). (41:10)

وَجَعَلَ فِيهَا رَوَٰسِىَ مِن فَوْقِهَا وَبَٰرَكَ فِيهَا وَقَدَّرَ فِيهَآ أَقْوَٰتَهَا فِىٓ أَرْبَعَةِ أَيَّامٍ سَوَآءً لِّلسَّآئِلِينَ ١٠

سورة فصلت: ١٠

Rawāsī, the plural of *rāsīyah*, is based on the verb *r-s-a*. Its verbal past tense is used for a ship moored at its berth (*rāsīyah* [berthed]), and its adjectival form as a noun denoting where a ship has been berthed or fixed. In *Arabic Dictionary*, arsa is said to mean "to anchor, moor, berth place at anchor" The word *rawāsī* is mentioned repeatedly in the Qur'an.

Or, who has made the earth firm to live in, made rivers in its midst, set on it *rawāsī*, and made a barrier between two bodies of flowing water? (Can there be another) god beside God. No, but most of them do not know. (27:61)

أَمَّن جَعَلَ ٱلْأَرْضَ قَرَارًا وَجَعَلَ خِلَٰلَهَآ أَنْهَٰرًا وَجَعَلَ لَهَا رَوَٰسِىَ وَجَعَلَ بَيْنَ ٱلْبَحْرَيْنِ حَاجِزًا أَءِلَٰهٌ مَّعَ ٱللَّهِ بَلْ أَكْثَرُهُمْ لَا يَعْلَمُونَ ٦١

سورة النمل: ٦١

We have spread out the earth (like a carpet), placed on it firm and *rawāsī*, and produced in it all kinds of things in due balance. (15:19)

وَٱلْأَرْضَ مَدَدْنَٰهَا وَأَلْقَيْنَا فِيهَا رَوَٰسِىَ وَأَنبَتْنَا فِيهَا مِن كُلِّ شَىْءٍ مَّوْزُونٍ ١٩

سورة الحجر: ١٩

God spread out the earth, set
on it *rawāsī* and flowing
rivers. He made all kinds of
fruit in two pairs, two and two.
He draws the night as a veil
over the day. Truly, in these
things are signs for those who
consider. (13:3)

وَهُوَ ٱلَّذِى مَدَّ ٱلْأَرْضَ وَجَعَلَ فِيهَا رَوَٰسِىَ وَأَنْهَٰرًا
وَمِن كُلِّ ٱلثَّمَرَٰتِ جَعَلَ فِيهَا زَوْجَيْنِ ٱثْنَيْنِ يُغْشِى ٱلَّيْلَ
ٱلنَّهَارَ إِنَّ فِى ذَٰلِكَ لَءَايَٰتٍ لِّقَوْمٍ يَتَفَكَّرُونَ ۝

سورة الرعد: ٣

God has stated that *rawāsī* have three distinct characteristics: they are
soaring or immense (77:27), they are there "lest the earth would cave in
and disappear from under us," an important characteristic mentioned
repeatedly (21:31; 16:15; 31:10), and they are cast on top of the earth
(4:10).

And made therein *rawāsī* that
are lofty (in stature), and provided for you sweet (and wholesome) water. (77:27)

وَجَعَلْنَا فِيهَا رَوَٰسِىَ شَٰمِخَٰتٍ وَأَسْقَيْنَٰكُم
مَّآءً فُرَاتًا ۝

سورة المرسلات: ٢٧

We have set on the earth
rawāsī, lest it should cave from
under you, and We have made
broad highways (between them)
for (people) to pass through and
so they may receive guidance.
(21:31)

وَجَعَلْنَا فِى ٱلْأَرْضِ رَوَٰسِىَ أَن تَمِيدَ بِهِمْ وَجَعَلْنَا
فِيهَا فِجَاجًا سُبُلًا لَّعَلَّهُمْ يَهْتَدُونَ ۝

سورة الأنبياء: ٣١

And He has set *rawāsī* on the
earth, lest it should cave from
under you, as well as rivers and
roads that you may guide yourselves. (16:15)

وَأَلْقَىٰ فِى ٱلْأَرْضِ رَوَٰسِىَ أَن تَمِيدَ بِكُمْ
وَأَنْهَٰرًا وَسُبُلًا لَّعَلَّكُمْ تَهْتَدُونَ ۝

سورة النحل: ١٥

He created the heavens without
visible pillars. He placed
rawāsī on the earth, lest it
should cave from under you,
and scattered throughout it all
kinds of beasts. We send rain
from the sky and produce on
the earth every kind of noble
kind (of life) to grow on earth.
(31:10)

خَلَقَ ٱلسَّمَٰوَٰتِ بِغَيْرِ عَمَدٍ تَرَوْنَهَا وَأَلْقَىٰ فِى ٱلْأَرْضِ
رَوَٰسِىَ أَن تَمِيدَ بِكُمْ وَبَثَّ فِيهَا مِن كُلِّ دَآبَّةٍ وَأَنزَلْنَا
مِنَ ٱلسَّمَآءِ مَآءً فَأَنۢبَتْنَا فِيهَا مِن كُلِّ زَوْجٍ
كَرِيمٍ ۝

سورة لقمان: ١٠

He placed *rawāsī* on the (earth), high above it, blessed the earth, and measured therein all things so that in four days they would receive nourishment in due proportion and in accordance with (the needs of) those who seek (sustenance). (41:10)

وَجَعَلَ فِيهَا رَوَاسِيَ مِن فَوْقِهَا وَبَارَكَ فِيهَا وَقَدَّرَ فِيهَآ أَقْوَاتَهَا فِىٓ أَرْبَعَةِ أَيَّامٍ سَوَآءً لِّلسَّآئِلِينَ ۝

سورة فصلت: ١٠

These three characteristics are very indicative of what modern science calls lithosphere plates, which are defined as geological formations that form the planet's outer layer and bear the continents and the oceans. The *Hutchinson Encyclopedia of the Earth* refers to it as the "skin of the earth." So, *rawāsī* are located on the planet's surface, which is the first characteristic mentioned by the Qur'an. Second, they are immense—74 kms. thick. They are there "lest the earth will cave from under us." The lithosphere's plates float on semimolten rock, as opposed to sinking beneath it, for they have been blocked at the edges by mountains. This will be discussed further in the coming pages.

As shown in figure 7, the earth is expanding, another fact that is mentioned repeatedly in the Qur'an.

And we have extended the earth and set on it *rawāsī*, and produced therein every kind of beautiful growth (in pairs). (50:7)

وَٱلْأَرْضَ مَدَدْنَٰهَا وَأَلْقَيْنَا فِيهَا رَوَٰسِيَ وَأَنبَتْنَا فِيهَا مِن كُلِّ زَوْجٍ بَهِيجٍ ۝

سورة ق: ٧

We have extended the earth out (like a carpet), set on it *rawāsī*, and produced in it all kinds of things in due balance. (15:19)

وَٱلْأَرْضَ مَدَدْنَٰهَا وَأَلْقَيْنَا فِيهَا رَوَٰسِيَ وَأَنبَتْنَا فِيهَا مِن كُلِّ شَىْءٍ مَّوْزُونٍ ۝

سورة الحجر: ١٩

However, our planet is being reduced from its extremities by subduction zones located at the points of plate interface. In the Qur'an, one reads:

Do they not see that We gradually curtail the land (under their control) from all its sides? God commands, and there is none to turn aside His command. He is swift to call (all) to account. (13:41)

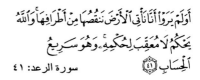

أَوَلَمْ يَرَوْاْ أَنَّا نَأْتِى ٱلْأَرْضَ نَنقُصُهَا مِنْ أَطْرَافِهَا وَٱللَّهُ يَحْكُمُ لَا مُعَقِّبَ لِحُكْمِهِۦ وَهُوَ سَرِيعُ ٱلْحِسَابِ ۝

سورة الرعد: ٤١

The disappearance of the continent-bearing *rawāsī* (lithosphere plates) would have continued if there had been no mountain ranges located on the leading edge of one plate, for these ranges act as a wedge between this point and the subduction zone of the opposing plate (fig. 12). In fact, this function of stopping the *rawāsī* from caving in is their most important role. God mentioned in the Qur'an that He made mountains to function as wedges or pegs.

And the mountains as pegs?
(78:7)

سورة النبأ: ٧ ۞ وَٱلْجِبَالَ أَوْتَادًا

The proof that mountains and *rawāsī* are not synonymous is found in Qur'an 79:32, which explains how mountains, in their role as wedges or pegs, were "berthed" at the *rawāsī*'s edges to stop the latter from sinking and disappearing into the interior. Such an event would destroy the affected continents and all forms of life thereon.

And He berthed the mountains.
(79:32)

سورة النازعات: ٣٢ ۞ وَٱلْجِبَالَ أَرْسَىٰهَا

A parallel can be drawn between the *rawāsī* and the plates of bone that form the human skull. The sutures between the bones, which appear on the human skull as a zigzag line, bear a marked resemblance to oceanic ridges and also allow the skull to grow without distorting its shape (fig. 13). Similarly, oceanic ridges allow the planet to expand under the

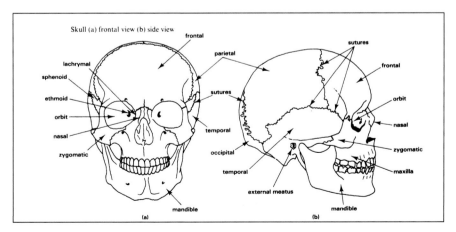

Figure 13: The similarity of the plates of bone that make up the skull and the earth's rawāsᵗ (lithosphere) plates.

ocean. Such growth produces horrific undersea volcanic eruptions that cannot be seen or felt on the surface. One can imagine that the *rawāsī* are like the bones that make up the skull. Just as the *rawāsī* protect the earth's interior by serving as a heat insulator, they also protect man from the interior's heat. This is similar to how the skull protects the human brain, eyes, and other organs from the heat, cold, and trauma of the environment. The suture between the bones of the skull closes at one year of age, but the *rawāsī* do not close, for the earth's interior is a sea of molten rock upon which the *rawāsī* continue to float and move at the rate of about half an inch per year. However, the *rawāsī* are so immense that their movement is felt only when a major earthquake takes place, such as those that shook San Francisco recently.

Figure 14 represents an assumed division of the earth into two sections. The one on the right passes through the Himalayan mountain range, which acts as a wedge or peg to prevent the plate carrying India from slipping under the plate carrying Asia. The section shows mountains functioning as wedges that prevent the lithosphere from disappearing into the earth, where it would melt and cause the destruction of the Indian subcontinent. The section on the left shows the Andes mountain range in South America, which

Figure 14: *Two sections through the earth. On the right, the Hima-layan mountain range stops the Indian subcontinent from disappearing into the earth. On the left, the Andes mountain range stops the South American plate from disappearing into the earth.*

is assumed to be unusually large—it is approximately 200-300 kms. deep and is considered one of the largest wedges in the world. It is situated at the top of the sinking Nazca oceanic plate and lies on top of the overriding South American lithospheric plate. Without this mountain range, South America would sink into the ocean and melt within the planet's interior.

To support what has been mentioned earlier, God describes how He is going to dismantle earth by reversing the process of creation. As mountains lock the *rawāsī* together, they will be the first to go. Then, He will move the mountains at such a speed that they will seem to be clouds, after which He will blow them up and cause them to vanish. Once the mountains or pegs are removed, the earth will seem to be protruding in places, a phenomenon that probably will be due to the separation of the lithosphere plates and the prominence of their edges.

One day We shall remove the mountains, and you will see the earth stretch as a level. We will gather them all together, and no one will be overlooked. (18:47)

وَيَوْمَ نُسَيِّرُ ٱلْجِبَالَ وَتَرَى ٱلْأَرْضَ بَارِزَةً وَحَشَرْنَٰهُمْ فَلَمْ نُغَادِرْ مِنْهُمْ أَحَدًا ﴿٤٧﴾

سورة الكهف : ٤٧

When the mountains vanish (like a mirage) ... (81:3)

وَإِذَا ٱلْجِبَالُ سُيِّرَتْ ﴿٣﴾

سورة التكوير : ٣

And the mountains will fly hither and thither. (52:10)

وَتَسِيرُ ٱلْجِبَالُ سَيْرًا ﴿١٠﴾

سورة الطور : ١٠

You see the mountains and think that they are fixed firmly. But they will pass away as clouds pass away. (Such is) the artistry of God, Who disposes of all things in perfect order, for He is well acquainted with all that you do. (27:88)

وَتَرَى ٱلْجِبَالَ تَحْسَبُهَا جَامِدَةً وَهِيَ تَمُرُّ مَرَّ ٱلسَّحَابِ صُنْعَ ٱللَّهِ ٱلَّذِي أَتْقَنَ كُلَّ شَيْءٍ إِنَّهُ خَبِيرٌ بِمَا تَفْعَلُونَ ﴿٨٨﴾

سورة النمل : ٨٨

And the mountains will vanish, as if they were a mirage. (78:20)

وَسُيِّرَتِ ٱلْجِبَالُ فَكَانَتْ سَرَابًا ﴿٢٠﴾

سورة النبأ : ٢٠

They ask you about the mountains. Say, "My Lord will uproot them and scatter them as dust." (20:105)

وَيَسْأَلُونَكَ عَنِ ٱلْجِبَالِ فَقُلْ يَنسِفُهَا رَبِّي نَسْفًا ﴿١٠٥﴾

سورة طه : ١٠٥

And the mountains shall be reduced to atoms. (56:5)

وَبُسَّتِ ٱلْجِبَالُ بَسًّا ۝

سورة الواقعة: ٥

And the mountains will be like
wool ... (70:9)

وَتَكُونُ ٱلْجِبَالُ كَٱلْعِهْنِ ۝

سورة المعارج: ٩

The Runaway Mountains

This was the title of a program broadcast on BBC2, London, on 11 December 1995. According to the laws of friction, when a vertical object falls,
the distance it will travel horizontally should be equal to its vertical height.
When runaway mountains collapse, however, they do not obey this law, for
the resulting debris can attain a speed of 70-120 mph and move 10 to 100
times the height of that part of the mountain in the process of collapse.

The first runaway mountain to be well documented, the Frank Landslide, was observed in 1903. The event involved the collapse of a 300 foot
mountainside located outside the mining town of Frank, Canada, and the
subsequent movement of the debris to a point two miles distant in only 100
seconds. It devastated the town and killed 70 people. The mountain did not
stop running until it reached a hill, which it then climbed for about 1 mile
before coming to a halt.

Sixty years later, Jim Moore of the United States Geological Survey
posited the existence of giant landslides and volcanic runaway mountains
while studying the Hawaiian islands. He believed that the northern part of
the island of Molokai and the northeast part of the island of Oahu were
missing due to prior collapse and runaway along the ocean bed. Supporting
evidence came from an old American navy deep-sea map that showed long
tails of debris spreading out along the ocean bed for many miles. His suggestion did not gain much support until detailed ocean-bed maps were
made in 1983, when the United States extended its territorial waters to 200
miles. A British ship surveyed the ocean with GLORIA (Geological Long
Range Inclined Asdic). Its signals, which were bounced off the sea floor to
produce an image (black representing sediments and white where the signal is reflected from rock), confirmed the existence of Moore's postulated
gigantic landslides.

The conclusive evidence for this theory was the runaway of Washington state's Mount St. Helens, in 1980. This was well documented by the
media and seen throughout the world. The mountainside began moving
over a meter per day one month before the runaway landslide and explosion. It ran away for a distance of 22 kilometers and caused a great deal of
devastation and casualties.

Since that incident, it has been discovered that runaway landslides occur every ten years somewhere in the world and in the European Alps every 100 years. In Japan, there are 100,000 areas of potential land sliding, which has caused that nation to set up a Disaster Prediction Research Institute to predict and study such catastrophes. It also publishes a journal, *Landslide News*, that reports on these events.

There are as many theories for the mechanisms of runaway mountains as there are investigators. The most prominent theory belongs to Ron Shreve (University of California, Los Angeles) who, in 1995, proposed that mountain debris is carried along on a cushion of compressed air. Another theory, that of acoustic fluidization, was proposed by Jay Melosh (University of Arizona). He made an experimental model to illustrate his contention that strong mechanical vibrations within the moving debris cause it to behave like a fluid. A third theory suggests that the top layers of debris move as one mass over the debris in the lower layers, which bounce and roll along the uneven ground as if they were rollers. Paul Cleary (Australian Commonwealth Scientific and Industrial Research Organization [Melbourne]), produced a computer simulation to illustrate this process.

Scientists in Hawaii are observing with concern and anxiety the great crack that divides the island. According to them, the internal pressure of the magma threatens to detach the southern part of the island along this fissure. According to Davin Calgue (Hawaiian Volcanic Observatory), such an event could cause a cascade of earthquakes and tidal waves. God only knows what its effect on our civilization would be.

Whatever the mechanism that allows mountains of any size to run away, it is only a modest example of what the Creator is capable of doing when He is ready to demolish earth.

Uplifting Mountains

God has asked people to reflect on how mountains were erected or uplifted (88:19). This precise description is used by contemporary scientists to describe the mechanisms by which mountains were created. There are three main types of mountains: fault-block, upwarped, and fold. Regardless of the formative mechanism, the resultant force always leads to the erection or upliftment of part of the earth or of its crust above the surface.

Fault-block mountains are the result of tensional stress resulting from continental drift. The tension can fracture (crack) rocks and thus produces long faults. Some blocks of land sink between parallel fault lines and create steep-sided rift valleys, such as the great East African rift valley. In other places, blocks of land are forced upward between faults and produce block mountains. The Sierra Nevada mountains in the United States and the Ruwenzori range west of the East African rift valley are examples of block mountains. Upwarped mountains, by contrast, are the result of compression that forces the upliftment of the crust. Examples include the southern Rocky Mountains and the Black Hills of the Dakotas. Fold mountains are formed by tremendous horizontal pressure that buckles rock layers into folds and thus causes their upliftment in the shape of a mountain. These are the largest and most complex of all mountain belts. In addition, they are compressional, for they result from the processes of folding, faulting, metamorphism, and igneous activity that result from the collision of lithosphere plates. The Himalayas are a spectacular example of fold mountains still in the process of formation, whereas the Urals are an example of ones that caused the rise long ago.

Do they not look at the how camels are made, how the sky is raised high, how the mountains are uplifted, and how the earth is spread out? (88:17-20)	أَفَلَا يَنظُرُونَ إِلَى ٱلْإِبِلِ كَيْفَ خُلِقَتْ ۝ وَإِلَى ٱلسَّمَآءِ كَيْفَ رُفِعَتْ ۝ وَإِلَى ٱلْجِبَالِ كَيْفَ نُصِبَتْ ۝ وَإِلَى ٱلْأَرْضِ كَيْفَ سُطِحَتْ ۝ سورة الغاشية: ١٧-٢٠

Earth's Surface

God spread the earth out so that life would be possible for His creatures (51:48). He uses the word *dahāhā* to describe how He spread it out and made it flat. The use of such a word is significant, for it describes an action similar to that of a grinding stone. This indicates that creation demanded a lot of grinding action similar to that of heavy rain, glacial and wind erosion, frost, and other natural phenomenon. Rocks picked up and held by ice enable a glacier to act as a powerful scraping agent, while a process of freezing and thawing is seen in deserts and other areas with extremes of temperature. In that environment, rocks expand during the heat of the day and contract during the cool of the night, and are eventually shattered (79:30).

We have spread out the (spacious earth. How excellently We have made it a resting place. (51:48)	وَٱلْأَرْضَ فَرَشْنَٰهَا فَنِعْمَ ٱلْمَٰهِدُونَ ۝ سورة الذاريات: ٤٨

After that We grounded the earth. (79:30)

سورة النازعات: ٣٠ وَٱلْأَرْضَ بَعْدَ ذَٰلِكَ دَحَىٰهَآ ۝

Creation of the Plant and Animal Kingdoms

The creation of the food and nourishment required by all creatures to sustain life took twice as long as that required for the creation of the earth. The length of time indicates how vast the task must have been.

He placed on the (earth) mountains that stand firm and high above it. He blessed the earth and measured all things therein so that they would receive their nourishment in due proportion, in four days, according to (the needs of) those who seek (sustenance). (41:10)

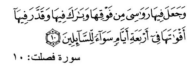

سورة فصلت: ١٠

The Creation of Plants

Plants are the most successful forms of life. There are some 350,000 different species ranging from the very large (e.g., forest trees) to the very small (e.g., moss, mold, and bacteria). They are found in almost every part of the world, even in freezing tundra, hot springs, or at high altitudes. Almost all are self-sufficient and can make their own food from elementary materials extracted from the air and the soil. Without them, animals and man could not exist, for plants replenish the planet's oxygen stores and offer themselves as food for many creatures.

God created the rivers and made each type of fruit in pairs, which gives evidence of reproduction. He describes the various types of plants, vines, palms, and others; states that they are all different, even though they are all irrigated with the same water (13:3-4); and invites man to study their differences. They are all made out of water (21:30), for God made all forms of life out of water, and then are irrigated with the same water. This raises a question: What factors decide the differences in their appearance and taste?

In fact, He was asking man to study the plant kingdom. Genetic studies of plants is far easier to conduct than those involved with animals and man. Early Mendelian laws of genetics were studied in plants and later extended to man. Researching plants involves no risk and is relatively inexpensive. It is also easy to reproduce the results, as the short life span of some plants makes it possible to study several generations in a short period of time.

God spread out the earth, set on it firm mountains and flowing rivers. He made all kinds of fruit in two pairs, two and two. He draws the night as a veil over the day. Truly, in these things are signs for those who consider. In the earth are neighboring (but diverse) tracts, gardens of vines, fields sown with corn, and palm trees growing out of single roots or otherwise, watered with the same water, yet some of them We make more excellent to eat than others. Truly in these things are signs for those who understand. (13:3-4)

وَهُوَ ٱلَّذِى مَدَّ ٱلْأَرْضَ وَجَعَلَ فِيهَا رَوَٰسِىَ وَأَنْهَٰرًا وَمِن كُلِّ ٱلثَّمَرَٰتِ جَعَلَ فِيهَا زَوْجَيْنِ ٱثْنَيْنِ يُغْشِى ٱلَّيْلَ ٱلنَّهَارَ إِنَّ فِى ذَٰلِكَ لَءَايَٰتٍ لِّقَوْمٍ يَتَفَكَّرُونَ ۝ وَفِى ٱلْأَرْضِ قِطَعٌ مُّتَجَٰوِرَٰتٌ وَجَنَّٰتٌ مِّنْ أَعْنَٰبٍ وَزَرْعٌ وَنَخِيلٌ صِنْوَانٌ وَغَيْرُ صِنْوَانٍ يُسْقَىٰ بِمَاءٍ وَٰحِدٍ وَنُفَضِّلُ بَعْضَهَا عَلَىٰ بَعْضٍ فِى ٱلْأُكُلِ إِنَّ فِى ذَٰلِكَ لَءَايَٰتٍ لِّقَوْمٍ يَعْقِلُونَ ۝

سورة الرعد: ٣-٤

Do the unbelievers not see that the heavens and the earth were joined together (as one unit of creation) before we caused them to separate? We made every living thing from water. Will they still not believe? (21:30)

أَوَلَمْ يَرَ ٱلَّذِينَ كَفَرُوٓا۟ أَنَّ ٱلسَّمَٰوَٰتِ وَٱلْأَرْضَ كَانَتَا رَتْقًا فَفَتَقْنَٰهُمَا وَجَعَلْنَا مِنَ ٱلْمَآءِ كُلَّ شَىْءٍ حَىٍّ أَفَلَا يُؤْمِنُونَ ۝

سورة الأنبياء: ٣٠

Not only did God say that He made all plants from pairs, but He also explained how He causes some of them to reproduce by air-borne fertilization. He commands the wind to carry pollen to plants that otherwise could not reproduce. It is now well known that this is the only way to fertilize several plants. Some plants, such as conifers, generally use the wind rather than insects for pollination purposes.

We send the fertilizing winds and then cause rain to fall from the sky, thereby providing you with (abundant) water, although you are not the guardians of its stores. (15:22)

وَأَرْسَلْنَا ٱلرِّيَٰحَ لَوَٰقِحَ فَأَنزَلْنَا مِنَ ٱلسَّمَآءِ مَآءً فَأَسْقَيْنَٰكُمُوهُ وَمَآ أَنتُمْ لَهُۥ بِخَٰزِنِينَ ۝

سورة الحجر: ٢٢

River Estuaries

One example of God's supreme power is His creation of rivers and seas. Although they mix with one another, on one side an individual can drink sweet water and, a few meters away, he can drink bitter salty water. In spite of this, the sea never flows into the rivers. He explains this by saying that He erected a barrier between them so that one would not overwhelm the other. This phenomenon is now well understood.

God is the one who caused two bodies of water to flow, one palpable and sweet, the other salty and bitter. He placed a barrier between them, a partition that they are forbidden to surmount. (25:53)

وَهُوَ ٱلَّذِى مَرَجَ ٱلْبَحْرَيْنِ هَٰذَا عَذْبٌ فُرَاتٌ وَهَٰذَا مِلْحٌ أُجَاجٌ وَجَعَلَ بَيْنَهُمَا بَرْزَخًا وَحِجْرًا مَّحْجُورًا ۝

سورة الفرقان: ٥٣

He causes two bodies of water to flow and meet together, but between them is a barrier that they cannot surmount. (55:19-20)

مَرَجَ ٱلْبَحْرَيْنِ يَلْتَقِيَانِ ۝
بَيْنَهُمَا بَرْزَخٌ لَّا يَبْغِيَانِ ۝   سورة الرحمن: ١٩-٢٠

Or, who has made the earth firm to live in, made rivers in its midst, set on it immovable mountains, and made a barrier between two bodies of flowing water? (Can there be another) god beside God. No, but most of them do not know. (27:61)

أَمَّن جَعَلَ ٱلْأَرْضَ قَرَارًا وَجَعَلَ خِلَٰلَهَآ أَنْهَٰرًا وَجَعَلَ لَهَا رَوَٰسِىَ وَجَعَلَ بَيْنَ ٱلْبَحْرَيْنِ حَاجِزًا أَءِلَٰهٌ مَّعَ ٱللَّهِ بَلْ أَكْثَرُهُمْ لَا يَعْلَمُونَ ۝

سورة النمل: ٦١

Figure 15:
A model of esturaine circulation.

Nor are the two bodies of flowing water alike, for one is palat-
able, sweet, and pleasant to
drink, while the other is salty
and bitter. Yet from each you
eat fresh and tender meat and
extract ornaments to wear. You
see ships therein that sail
through the waves that you
may seek the bounty of God
and be grateful. (35:12)

وَمَا يَسْتَوِي الْبَحْرَانِ هَٰذَا عَذْبٌ فُرَاتٌ سَآئِغٌ
شَرَابُهُۥ وَهَٰذَا مِلْحٌ أُجَاجٌ وَمِن كُلٍّ تَأْكُلُونَ لَحْمًا
طَرِيًّا وَتَسْتَخْرِجُونَ حِلْيَةً تَلْبَسُونَهَا وَتَرَى
الْفُلْكَ فِيهِ مَوَاخِرَ لِتَبْتَغُوا مِن فَضْلِهِۦ
وَلَعَلَّكُمْ تَشْكُرُونَ ﴿١٢﴾

سورة فاطر: ١٢

Science only became aware of this phenomenon after the satellite
Gemini 4 photographed the Nile Delta during 3-7 June 1965. The barrier
between the river and the sea, which was described by God nearly fourteen
centuries ago, is now known as estuarine circulation. The river transports
three major types of material: fresh water, dissolved organic and inorganic
substances, and such detritus as organic material, sand, silt, or clay (which
helps to shape the coastline). Large rivers, such as the Nile, acquire a high
speed during their journey toward the sea and, due to the resulting turbu-
lence, carry a sizeable suspended load of clay, silt, and sand. The sudden
change in velocity makes the sediment to drop out rapidly. Moreover, the
colloidal clay fraction is coagulated by the salty water, which helps further
sedimentation.

Most rivers debouch onto a continental shelf, which results in the formation of a delta that is usually located at the river's mouth. As fresh
water flows into the ocean, it tends to ride over the denser salty sea water.
The two waters begin to mix, albeit slowly, as the fresh water goes further out into the sea. Since the river's water is added to the sea's surface,
it tends to flow out slowly. To balance the loss of sea water due to river
discharge on the surface, a supply of higher-density sea water flows
beneath the surface and toward the river mouth. This is known as estuarine circulation (fig. 15), a process that consists of pushing sediment
toward the continents to form, over time, deltas or build up the shoreline.
This is how we understand the "barrier" God created between fresh water
and sea water.

Most people do not realize that the creation of the heavens and the
earth is greater than that of man (55:57). He did not create "the heavens and the earth and what is between them to play" (21:16). He knows
their secrets (25:6), for they belong to Him (20:5-6). There is much to
learn from the creation of the heavens and the earth, which is why God

asked man to reflect on how all this has been made subservient to him (2:164).

Truly the creation of the heavens and the earth is a greater (matter) than the creation of mankind. But most of them do not understand. (40:57)

لَخَلْقُ ٱلسَّمَوَٰتِ وَٱلْأَرْضِ أَكْبَرُ مِنْ خَلْقِ ٱلنَّاسِ وَلَٰكِنَّ أَكْثَرَ ٱلنَّاسِ لَا يَعْلَمُونَ ۝

سورة غافر: ٥٧

We did not create the heavens and the earth and all that is between them for (idle) sport. (21:16)

وَمَا خَلَقْنَا ٱلسَّمَآءَ وَٱلْأَرْضَ وَمَا بَيْنَهُمَا لَٰعِبِينَ ۝

سورة الأنبياء: ١٦

Say: "The (Qur'an) was sent down by God, who knows the secret (that is) in the heavens and the earth. Truly, He is Oft-Forgiving, Most Merciful. (25:6)

قُلْ أَنزَلَهُ ٱلَّذِى يَعْلَمُ ٱلسِّرَّ فِى ٱلسَّمَوَٰتِ وَٱلْأَرْضِ إِنَّهُۥ كَانَ غَفُورًا رَّحِيمًا ۝

سورة الفرقان: ٦

(God) Most Gracious is firmly established on the throne (of authority). To Him belongs what is in the heavens and on the earth, as well as what is between them and beneath the soil. (20:5-6)

ٱلرَّحْمَٰنُ عَلَى ٱلْعَرْشِ ٱسْتَوَىٰ ۝ لَهُۥ مَا فِى ٱلسَّمَوَٰتِ وَمَا فِى ٱلْأَرْضِ وَمَا بَيْنَهُمَا وَمَا تَحْتَ ٱلثَّرَىٰ ۝

سورة طه: ٥-٦

Behold! In the creation of the heavens and the earth, in the alternation of night and day, in the sailing of ships through the ocean for the profit of man-kind, in the rain that God sends from the skies and the life that He gives thereby to a dead earth, in the beasts of all kinds that He scatters throughout the earth, in the change of the winds and the clouds that trail them like slaves between the sky and the earth—(Here) indeed are signs for people who are wise. (2:164)

إِنَّ فِى خَلْقِ ٱلسَّمَوَٰتِ وَٱلْأَرْضِ وَٱخْتِلَٰفِ ٱلَّيْلِ وَٱلنَّهَارِ وَٱلْفُلْكِ ٱلَّتِى تَجْرِى فِى ٱلْبَحْرِ بِمَا يَنفَعُ ٱلنَّاسَ وَمَآ أَنزَلَ ٱللَّهُ مِنَ ٱلسَّمَآءِ مِن مَّآءٍ فَأَحْيَا بِهِ ٱلْأَرْضَ بَعْدَ مَوْتِهَا وَبَثَّ فِيهَا مِن كُلِّ دَآبَّةٍ وَتَصْرِيفِ ٱلرِّيَٰحِ وَٱلسَّحَابِ ٱلْمُسَخَّرِ بَيْنَ ٱلسَّمَآءِ وَٱلْأَرْضِ لَأَيَٰتٍ لِّقَوْمٍ يَعْقِلُونَ ۝

سورة البقرة: ١٦٤

The Hydrologic Cycle

God describes the hydrologic (water) cycle repeatedly in the Qur'an. He sends the wind, a merciful gesture of His hands, to bring up and to drive (transport) heavy laden clouds to dry areas and then drop their water (precipitation) on dry dead land in order to bring forth fruits of all kinds. This is how He brings forth life (7:57). He drops the water in a carefully measured quantity, causes it to remain inside the ground, and is also quite capable of taking it away (23:18). This is how ground water is formed and stored. Water falling from the sky threads its way (filtration) into the ground and emerges as springs (39:21). When the water table reaches the surface, the water rises from the ground and forms a spring. If this occurs in the desert, the spring will create a fertile spot (oasis). Some of the world's greatest rivers develop from springs.

As shown earlier, rivers flow into the sea or ocean and salty water does not flow back into rivers (15:53). Ground water is the second greatest store (8.4×10^{15} cm.) of water after oceans (1350×10^{15} cm.), and glaciers and polar ice (29×10^{15} cm.). Lakes and rivers come third (0.2×10^{15} cm.). Ground water is extremely valuable, is protected from evaporation, and moves slowly over years rather than days. Unfortunately, it becomes hot enough at a certain depth to dissolve salts. As a result, only about 8 percent of all ground water is useful for human, plant, or animal use. For an exceedingly wet planet, Earth has little water that can be easily used. Less than one millionth of all surface water is fresh and located in streams and rivers—a hundred times more is held in lakes.

God made all forms of life on Earth from water. He stressed its importance by saying that "His throne was on the water."

God sends the winds like heralds of glad tidings going before His mercy. When they have carried the heavy-laden clouds, we drive them to a dead land, cause rain to fall on it, and produce every kind of harvest therewith. Thus shall We raise up the dead. Perhaps you will remember. (7:57)

وَهُوَ ٱلَّذِى يُرْسِلُ ٱلرِّيَٰحَ بُشْرًۢا بَيْنَ يَدَىْ رَحْمَتِهِۦ حَتَّىٰٓ إِذَآ أَقَلَّتْ سَحَابًا ثِقَالًا سُقْنَٰهُ لِبَلَدٍ مَّيِّتٍ فَأَنزَلْنَا بِهِ ٱلْمَآءَ فَأَخْرَجْنَا بِهِۦ مِن كُلِّ ٱلثَّمَرَٰتِ كَذَٰلِكَ نُخْرِجُ ٱلْمَوْتَىٰ لَعَلَّكُمْ تَذَكَّرُونَ ۝

سورة الأعراف: ٥٧

Do you not see that God sends rain from the sky, leads it through springs in the earth, and then causes produce of various colors to grow and then wither? You will see it grow yellow, after which He makes it dry up and crumble away. Truly in this is a message of remembrance to men of understanding. (39:21)

أَلَمْ تَرَ أَنَّ ٱللَّهَ أَنزَلَ مِنَ ٱلسَّمَآءِ مَآءً فَسَلَكَهُ يَنَٰبِيعَ فِى ٱلْأَرْضِ ثُمَّ يُخْرِجُ بِهِۦ زَرْعًا مُّخْتَلِفًا أَلْوَٰنُهُۥ ثُمَّ يَهِيجُ فَتَرَىٰهُ مُصْفَرًّا ثُمَّ يَجْعَلُهُۥ حُطَٰمًا إِنَّ فِى ذَٰلِكَ لَذِكْرَىٰ لِأُو۟لِى ٱلْأَلْبَٰبِ ۝

سورة الزمر: ٢١

We send water from the sky according to (due) measure and cause it to soak into the soil. Certainly, We can drain it off (easily). (23:18)

وَأَنزَلْنَا مِنَ ٱلسَّمَآءِ مَآءً بِقَدَرٍ فَأَسْكَنَّٰهُ فِى ٱلْأَرْضِ وَإِنَّا عَلَىٰ ذَهَابٍ بِهِۦ لَقَٰدِرُونَ ۝

سورة المؤمنون: ١٨

CHAPTER FOUR

CREATION OF THE ANIMAL KINGDOM

General Account

Animals range from primitive microscopic protozoa to giant 95-foot-long blue whales weighing up to 100 tons. There are animals that fly in the air; swim in the seas, rivers, and lakes; and crawl, walk, run, hop, and climb on the ground and in the soil. There are well over one million different varieties. The largest group is that of the insects (more than 800,000 varieties), which is followed by fish (about 30,000 varieties), birds (9,000 varieties), reptiles (6,000 varieties), and mammals (5,000 varieties).

Each kind of animal has a different way of life and prefers a special type of environment: the bottom of the sea, the top of a mountain, deserts, trees, and grasslands. To make each creature suitable for its environment and perhaps for the education of man, God has demonstrated His creative skills sometimes in the most unusual ways. The North American daddy-longlegs, the ichneumon fly, has its ears in its feet so that it can listen for noises made by horn-tail wasp larvae when the latter is chewing wood. After they hatch, fly larvae can only live by eating wasp larvae. Thus, the female fly locates the wasp larvae with extreme accuracy by running up and down tree trunks listening, with the hearing cells in her feet, for chewing noises made by wasp larvae. Another unusual creation is found in Copilia quadrata, a shrimp-like creature, that lives in the bay of Naples. Its eyes have a lens but no retina. The picture light rays fall on a single light-sensitive spot that darts about and builds up an image as a system of dots. This is similar to the scanning function of a picture tube located inside a television receiver. The most unusual feature is that this shrimp's receiving equipment, which is equal to our brain, is located in its waist.

God provided many examples for man to watch and study. Although man has discovered electricity, our electric bulb only has an energy output of 4 percent light and 90 percent heat. A firefly produces light with such a bright glow that the amount of light produced by six large fireflies would produce enough light to enable a person to read a book. This light is produced by chemicals and enzymes combining with oxygen. Attempts to reproduce this "living light" or bioluminescence of animal life artificially has so far proved more expensive than the production of man-made electricity.

Animal Resurrection

A lot can be learned from the animal kingdom. Not only is it essential for man's existence, but it is also vital for his education. Therefore, it is not very fair to treat animals unkindly. If one imagines the number of different animal species mentioned above and how many of each kind have existed since creation began, the figure would be beyond comprehension. One has to think deeply in order to appreciate the fact that each species forms a nation like ourselves. However, the most amazing fact is that God is going to gather them to His presence. I hate to think what sort of complaints members of the animal kingdom will present to God concerning their treatment at the hands of man.

Each animal (that walks) on the earth or flies with wings (forms part of) communities like you. We have omitted nothing from the Book, and they shall be gathered to their Lord in the end. (6:38)

وَمَا مِن دَآبَّةٍ فِى ٱلْأَرْضِ وَلَا طَـٰٓئِرٍ يَطِيرُ بِجَنَاحَيْهِ إِلَّآ أُمَمٌ أَمْثَالُكُم مَّا فَرَّطْنَا فِى ٱلْكِتَبِ مِن شَىْءٍ ثُمَّ إِلَىٰ رَبِّهِمْ يُحْشَرُونَ ﴿٣٨﴾

سورة الأنعام : ٣٨

As mentioned earlier, God created every animal that "walks on the earth" out of water. Although their bodies are made mainly of water, He demonstrates His creative skill by varying their shape, size, structure, and appearance. It has been confirmed scientifically that the main bulk of an animal's body, as in a man and a plant, is made of water.

God has created every animal from water. Some crawl on their stomachs, some walk on two legs, and some walk on four (legs). God creates what He wills, for truly He has power over everything. (24:45)

وَٱللَّهُ خَلَقَ كُلَّ دَآبَّةٍ مِّن مَّآءٍ فَمِنْهُم مَّن يَمْشِى عَلَىٰ بَطْنِهِ وَمِنْهُم مَّن يَمْشِى عَلَىٰ رِجْلَيْنِ وَمِنْهُم مَّن يَمْشِى عَلَىٰٓ أَرْبَعٍ يَخْلُقُ ٱللَّهُ مَا يَشَآءُ إِنَّ ٱللَّهَ عَلَىٰ كُلِّ شَىْءٍ قَدِيرٌ ﴿٤٥﴾

سورة النور : ٤٥

People who claim, falsely, that God has prohibited certain animal meats while allowing others for economic gain will not be successful.

Do not say, falsely, "This is lawful, and that is forbidden," and thus ascribe what is false to God, for those who do so will never prosper. (16:116)

وَلَا تَقُولُوا لِمَا تَصِفُ أَلْسِنَتُكُمُ الْكَذِبَ
هَٰذَا حَلَٰلٌ وَهَٰذَا حَرَامٌ لِّتَفْتَرُوا عَلَى اللَّهِ الْكَذِبَ
إِنَّ الَّذِينَ يَفْتَرُونَ عَلَى اللَّهِ الْكَذِبَ لَا يُفْلِحُونَ ١١٦

Prohibited Meat

سورة النحل: ١١٦

God has prohibited, for reasons which will be explained shortly, the consumption of carrion, blood, pork, and the meat of animals that have been strangled, beaten, fallen (to their deaths), gored, and devoured by beasts of prey. This would have sounded extremely mysterious and perhaps unacceptable fourteen centuries ago, but today at least 175 pathogenic micro-organisms are known to cause disease in the non-human world. These diseases are referred to as *zoonoses*. Table 1 lists some of the diseases transmitted from animal to man, the causative agent, and the mode of transmittal. If one were to comment on each disease, an entire textbook of medicine would be the result.

Diseased animals, whether dead or alive, contain these micro-organisms in their blood and other organs. Animals that have been beaten or bitten by beasts of prey may be incubating or suffering from diseases transmitted by biting, such as rabies. Moreover, the corpses of dead animals are usually taken over and soon colonized by micro-organisms. Blood, which harbors bacteria and their toxins, viruses, chemicals, poisons, and so on, would be very harmful if consumed by humans. The wisdom of this verse is now well understood.

Diseases Transmitted Directly or Indirectly from Animals to Man

Mode of transmission			
Disease	**Pathogen**	**Ingestion**	**Contact**
Viral			
Contagious ecythyma (orf)	Parapoxvirus		+
Eastern hemisphere tick-borne encephalitis	Flavivirus	+	
Hemorragic fever, ARDS	Hantavirus	+	+
Lassa fever	Arenavirus		+
LCM meningitis	Lymphocytic choriomeningitis	+	
Milker's nodule	Parapoxvirus		+
Omsk hemorragic fever	Flavivirus		+

Powassan virus encephalitis	Flavivirus	+	
Rabies	Rhabdovirus		+
Rift Valley fever	Phlebovirus	+	+

Bacterial

Anthrax	Bacillus anthracis	+	+
Brucellosis	Brucella spp.	+	+
Campylobacteriosis	Campylobacter jejuni	+	
Cat scratch disease	Rochalimaea henselae		+
Cholera	Vibrio cholerae	+	
Edwardsiella infection	Edwardsiella tarda	+	
Erysipeloid	Erysipelothrix rhusiopathiae		+
Gastrenteritis	Vibrio parahaemolyticus	+	
Glanders	Pseudomonas mallei	+	+
Leptospirosis	Leptospira interrogans spp.	+	+
Listeriosis	Listeria monocytogenes	+	
Pasteurellosis	Pasteurella multocida		+
Plague	Yersinia pestis		+
Plesiomonas gastroenteritis	Plesiomonas shigelloides	+	
Rat bite fever (H)	Streptobacillus moniliformis	+	+
Rat bite fever (S)	Spirillum minus		+
Rocky Mountain spotted fever	Rickettsia reckettsii		+
Salmonellosis	Salmonella enteriditis	+	
Septicemia-canine bite associated	Capnocytophaga canimorsus	+	
Skin gangrene sepsis-salt water	Vibrio vulnificus	+	+
Tuberculosis	Mycobacterium bovis	+	
Tularemia	Francisella tularensis	+	+
Yeriniosis	Yersinia enterocolitica	+	
Yersiniosis	Yersinia pseudotuberculosis	+	

Parasitic

Angiostrongyliasis	Parastrongylus cantonensis	+	+
Cyclospora infection	Cyclospora spp.	+	
Climorchiasis	Clonorchis sinensis	+	
Crytosporidiosis	Cryptosporidia spp.	+	
Cysticercosis	Taenia solium	+	
Echinococcosis	Echinococcus granulosis	+	
Fascioliasis	Fasciola hepatica	+	
Giardiasis	Giardia lamblia	+	
Paragonimiasis	Paragonimus	+	
Toxocariasis	Toxocara canis, cati		+
Toxoplasmosis	Toxoplasma gondii	+	
Trichinosis	Trichinella spiralis	+	

God also emphasized that animals must not be abused and so forbade the consumption of the flesh of animals used in idolatrous sacrificial or divination rituals. Even more respect and consideration was given to animals destined to be sacrificied according to Islamic norms, as Muslims consider this deed sacred. The name of God as well as a small prayer should be mentioned before and during the sacrifice. Perhaps when such an animal is gathered to Him on the Day of Judgment, it will be rewarded for offering itself to man. An example of this sacred ritual will be given later.

The following foods are forbidden: corpses, blood, pork, the flesh of animals over which the name of something other than God has been invoked; the meat of animals killed by strangulation, a violent blow, a headlong fall, a fatal goring; or the flesh of an animal that has been consumed (partially) by a wild animal. Save that which you (yourselves) may have slaughtered while it was still alive, and all animals sacrificed on stone (altars) are forbidden, as are those whose corpses are used in divining rituals. That is impiety. This day, those who reject faith have given up all hope of your religion. Do not fear them, but fear Me. This day, I have perfected your religion for you, completed My favor upon you, and have chosen for you Islam as your religion. If one is forced by hunger and does not intend to transgress, God is indeed Oft-Forgiving, Most Merciful. (5:3)

حُرِّمَتۡ عَلَيۡكُمُ ٱلۡمَيۡتَةُ وَٱلدَّمُ وَلَحۡمُ ٱلۡخِنزِيرِ وَمَآ أُهِلَّ لِغَيۡرِ ٱللَّهِ بِهِۦ وَٱلۡمُنۡخَنِقَةُ وَٱلۡمَوۡقُوذَةُ وَٱلۡمُتَرَدِّيَةُ وَٱلنَّطِيحَةُ وَمَآ أَكَلَ ٱلسَّبُعُ إِلَّا مَا ذَكَّيۡتُمۡ وَمَا ذُبِحَ عَلَى ٱلنُّصُبِ وَأَن تَسۡتَقۡسِمُوا۟ بِٱلۡأَزۡلَٰمِ ذَٰلِكُمۡ فِسۡقٌ ٱلۡيَوۡمَ يَئِسَ ٱلَّذِينَ كَفَرُوا۟ مِن دِينِكُمۡ فَلَا تَخۡشَوۡهُمۡ وَٱخۡشَوۡنِ ٱلۡيَوۡمَ أَكۡمَلۡتُ لَكُمۡ دِينَكُمۡ وَأَتۡمَمۡتُ عَلَيۡكُمۡ نِعۡمَتِى وَرَضِيتُ لَكُمُ ٱلۡإِسۡلَٰمَ دِينٗا فَمَنِ ٱضۡطُرَّ فِى مَخۡمَصَةٍ غَيۡرَ مُتَجَانِفٖ لِّإِثۡمٖ فَإِنَّ ٱللَّهَ غَفُورٞ رَّحِيمٌ ۝

سورة المائدة: ٣

Taenia Solium and Human Cysticercosis

Pork has been forbidden for a very good reason—it was common for swine to be infected with the tapeworm taenia solium. This infection must have been very prevalent in the past, for it has proven very difficult to control even now with all of our advanced knowledge. It can be found throughout the world, especially in eastern Europe, Central and South America, Spain, Portugal, parts of Africa, China, and India.

Taenia solium is only one of the tapeworms that can infect man. Taenia saginata is present in cattle. Both tapeworms cause an illness in man that follows the two stages of their life cycle. The adult stage produces gastro-intestinal symptoms in man, who happens to be the definitive host for the adult tapeworm, as the human body allows the tapeworm's full development. In its larval stages, the tapeworm penetrates the intestinal mucosa and survives in the tissues for varying periods of time. Unfortunately, the human body can support the larva or intermediate stage (Echinococcus granulosus) of the taenia solium tapeworm that is present in pigs.

The tapeworm's life cycle (fig. 16) starts with eating diseased or in-fected pork that contains the larvae in an encysted form (Cysticercus). This larvae is a fluid-filled sac that contains the head and has a diameter of only a few centimeters. When cyst-infected pork is consumed, the cysts will hatch and the larvae will cling to the intestine by its head or scolex, which is designed for attachment by a rostellum surrounded by a group of hooks (fig. 17). The rest of the body can grow up to 10 or 20 feet in length. The head leads to a short neck, after which comes the rest of the body, which is divided into segments (proglottids) containing both male and female repro-ductive organs. Eggs are formed, fertilized, and then either released into the intestine or the segments are expelled, as a whole, through the feces. Both eggs and segments can be found in human feces. When they are eaten by an intermediate host (e.g., pigs, dogs, cats), the eggs will develop into lar-vae that migrate through the pig's intestine to its muscles and other organs.

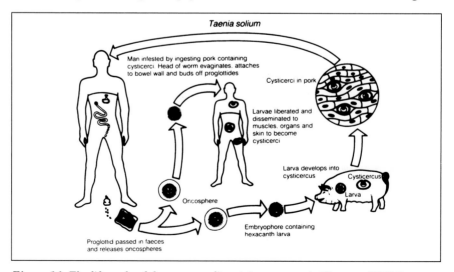

Figure 16: *The life cycle of the taenea solium (pig tapeworm). (Courtesy WTIM).*

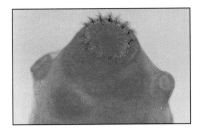

Figure 17:.Taenea solium (pig tapeworm or armed tapeworm). Scolex showing hooklets.

Human cysticercosis is caused through contact with human feces that contain taenia solium eggs. One can be infected through food or water that has been contaminated by human feces or if one's mouth comes into contact with the anus of an individual whose body carries an adult worm. Reverse peristalsis of the intestine may also cause internal infection. The intermediate stage (cysticercus cellulosae) involves the egg's hatching, the larva's penetration of the intestinal wall, and its transformation into a cyst containing a head. The cyst is 0.5-1 cm in diameter and remains viable for three to five years, after which it becomes calcified. Figure 18 shows an X-ray of such calcified cysts in the muscles of a patient's arms. Although these cysts can develop in almost any part of the body, they usually affect the cerebrum, the subarachnoid space at the base of the brain, and the ventricles. The infected individual will suffer from headaches, paralysis, partial blindness, and epilepsy. It may also affect the eye, heart, liver, and spleen.

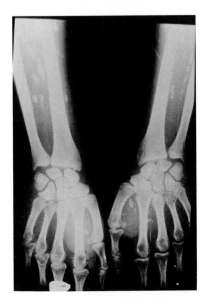

Figure 18: An X-ray showing the arm bones of a patient infected with calcified human cysticercosis.The cysts are the dense shadows in between the bones of the hand and the arm.

Other Prohibited Meats

An animal that has been "strangled, beaten, gored, devoured by other beasts, or has fallen to death" should be treated by man as a dead animal whose injuries might contain health-threatening infections. However, despite the above command not to consume the meat of dying or infected animals or their corpses, common sense prevails. If, for example, an individual is facing starvation in the middle of the desert or under other pressing circumstances, he can eat whatever meat is available in order to save his life.

He has only forbidden (the consumption) of corpses, blood, pork, and food over which the name of something other than God has been invoked. But if one is forced by necessity, and not by willful disobedience or (desire) to transgress due limits, God is Oft-Forgiving, Most Merciful. (16:115)	إِنَّمَا حَرَّمَ عَلَيْكُمُ ٱلْمَيْتَةَ وَٱلدَّمَ وَلَحْمَ ٱلْخِنزِيرِ وَمَآ أُهِلَّ لِغَيْرِ ٱللَّهِ بِهِۦ فَمَنِ ٱضْطُرَّ غَيْرَ بَاغٍ وَلَا عَادٍ فَإِنَّ ٱللَّهَ غَفُورٌ رَّحِيمٌ ﴿١١٥﴾ سورة النحل: ١١٥

Animals and birds that have been trained by man to hunt usually do not hurt their prey, and so God has allowed man to eat animals caught in this manner, provided that the same sacrificial ritual is observed.

They ask you what (food) is lawful. Say: All things that are good and pure, and what you have taught your trained hunting animals (to catch), as God has directed. Eat what they catch for you, but pronounce the name of God over it and fear Him, for God takes account swiftly (5:4)	يَسْـَٔلُونَكَ مَاذَآ أُحِلَّ لَهُمْ قُلْ أُحِلَّ لَكُمُ ٱلطَّيِّبَـٰتُ وَمَا عَلَّمْتُم مِّنَ ٱلْجَوَارِحِ مُكَلِّبِينَ تُعَلِّمُونَهُنَّ مِمَّا عَلَّمَكُمُ ٱللَّهُ فَكُلُوا۟ مِمَّآ أَمْسَكْنَ عَلَيْكُمْ وَٱذْكُرُوا۟ ٱسْمَ ٱللَّهِ عَلَيْهِ وَٱتَّقُوا۟ ٱللَّهَ إِنَّ ٱللَّهَ سَرِيعُ ٱلْحِسَابِ ﴿٤﴾ سورة المائدة: ٤

The Islamic Ritual of Animal Sacrifice

The ceremony starts with saying "In the name of God, the Beneficent, the Merciful." A short prayer is then said, both before and during the actual sacrifice, asking God to give the animal patience in its plight. Observing this ritual makes the meat religiously clean and pure (ḥalāl), for it follows the guidelines of sacrificing animals in a humane manner and with a minimum of pain. The method also clears the slaughtered animal's corpse of any circulating toxins, bacteria, viruses, and parasites by means of cutting the jugular veins on either side of its neck (the method of choice). This action cuts the supply of blood to the brain instantly, so the animal will feel no pain. It also allows the heart to continue beating and thus empty the tissues and circulatory network of blood. The blood will drain from the area where the veins were severed, which will clear the muscles and internal organs of blood and possible harmful material. It will also remove the "wild" taste found in animals sacrificed by other techniques, which has led many people to become vegetarians.

The Production of Milk

Another small anatomical lesson showing God's creative power is illustrated by the production of milk from cattle. As such cattle-borne diseases as brucellosis can be transmitted through milk, it has to be boiled or pasteurized. Milk is favored by man at all stages of his development. It is fascinating how God extracts such a delicious fluid from specific parts, which are filled with blood and excreta, of milk-producing animals. We now know that milk is produced by a specialized organ: the mammary gland. This gland consists of lactiferous lobes and lobules that lead to the lactiferous ducts that, in turn, open at the nipple or teat. The lobes and lobules of this gland contain excretory cells that produce milk. The mammary gland receives the necessary blood and lymphatic supply from the body, which carries all of the nutrition required by the new-born animal.

You will also find an instructive sign in cattle, as regards what is within their bodies. In between (their) excretions and blood, We produce milk that is pure and agreeable to those who drink it. (16:66)

وَإِنَّ لَكُمْ فِى ٱلْأَنْعَـٰمِ لَعِبْرَةً نُّسْقِيكُم مِّمَّا فِى بُطُونِهِۦ
مِنۢ بَيْنِ فَرْثٍ وَدَمٍ لَّبَنًا خَالِصًا
سَآئِغًا لِّلشَّـٰرِبِينَ ٦٦

سورة النحل: ٦٦

Transportation

For a long time, animals and boats were the only methods of transport known to man. However, God has referred to other possible (and as yet unknown) means of transport(16:8). The Qur'an refers to such means in a very mysterious way. In one instance, God vows by "the twilight, by the night and what it envelopes, and by the full moon as it grows to its fulness" and that you will ride and travel from stage to stage (84:16-19). Traditional explanations have no relation to transportation. As a matter of fact, nobody at that time could imagine such a means of transportation. I do not claim to know what it means, but only offer it as an example of what we do not know. However, it is stated in the Qur'an (17:1) that Muhammad was taken from Makkah to Jerusalem and returned to Makkah during the same night. This verse will be discussed later. People in the past would never have believed that anything could go faster than a horse or a wild animal. They had never heard about the spine-tailed swift, which has been reported to fly at speeds in excess of 200 mph. He who has created the spine-tailed swift is capable of taking man, with or without a machine, at any time to any place in space.

(He created) horses, mules, and donkeys for you to ride and use for show, and He has created (other) things about which you know nothing. (16:8)

وَٱلْخَيْلَ وَٱلْبِغَالَ وَٱلْحَمِيرَ لِتَرْكَبُوهَا وَزِينَةً وَيَخْلُقُ مَا لَا تَعْلَمُونَ ۝

سورة النحل: ٨

I call to witness the ruddy glow of the sunset, the night and its homing, and the moon in its fullness. You shall surely travel from stage to stage. (84:16-19)

فَلَا أُقْسِمُ بِٱلشَّفَقِ ۝ وَٱلَّيْلِ وَمَا وَسَقَ ۝ وَٱلْقَمَرِ إِذَا ٱتَّسَقَ ۝ لَتَرْكَبُنَّ طَبَقًا عَن طَبَقٍ ۝

سورة الانشقاق: ١٦-١٩

Glory be to God, Who took His servant for a night journey from the Sacred Mosque to the Farthest Mosque, whose precincts We have blessed, in order that We might show him some of Our signs, for He hears and sees (everything). (17:1)

سُبْحَٰنَ ٱلَّذِىٓ أَسْرَىٰ بِعَبْدِهِۦ لَيْلًا مِّنَ ٱلْمَسْجِدِ ٱلْحَرَامِ إِلَى ٱلْمَسْجِدِ ٱلْأَقْصَا ٱلَّذِى بَٰرَكْنَا حَوْلَهُۥ لِنُرِيَهُۥ مِنْ ءَايَٰتِنَآ إِنَّهُۥ هُوَ ٱلسَّمِيعُ ٱلْبَصِيرُ ۝

سورة الإسراء: ١

CHAPTER FIVE

CREATION OF THE SUPERNATURAL

Angels

The supernatural, by definition, must elude natural science no matter how perfect that science may be. Just because one cannot see angels does not mean that they do not exist. What is supernatural to man is certainly primitive for God. A well-programmed computer can work astronomical calculations as well as command robots to manufacture cars or handle radioactive material that cannot be touched. They are indispensable to modern life, for they control such functions as supplying electricity to cities, telephone networks, aircraft controls, spaceships, satellites, and so on.

Thus, it is not surprising that God would have creatures capable of handling all matters of the universe on His behalf. Such beings are called angels. They are different from man, for they can fly (35:1) and serve as messengers on God's behalf (22:75). Although they are "not suited to walk peacefully among human beings" (17:95), they nevertheless have numerous tasks to perform on Earth, some of which are related to us, and protect us with God's command (13:11; 82:10; 86:4). For example, one may just miss a plane, a bus, or a train only to learn later that it had been involved in an accident, or one may recover from a supposedly incurable illness and regain his health. On the other hand, one might be "lucky" and come into an unexpected fortune, find a treasure, or receive a large inheritance from a distant relative. Although such surprises are usually considered "good luck," others might think that heaven was involved. It seems that supernatural powers can have an effect on certain situations. Angels also seem to act as observers who note what one does, says, or thinks (43:80; 50:17-18).

Praise be to God, who created the heavens and the earth (out of nothing), Who made the

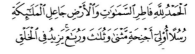

angels messengers with wings, two, or three, or four (pairs). He adds to creation as He pleases, for God has power over everything. (35:1)

مَا يَشَآءُ إِنَّ ٱللَّهَ عَلَىٰ كُلِّ شَىۡءٍ قَدِيرٌ ۝

سورة فاطر : ١

God chooses messengers from angels and from men, for He hears and sees (everything). (22:75)

ٱللَّهُ يَصۡطَفِى مِنَ ٱلۡمَلَـٰٓئِكَةِ رُسُلًا وَمِنَ ٱلنَّاسِ إِنَّ ٱللَّهَ سَمِيعٌ بَصِيرٌ ۝

سورة الحج : ٧٥

Say, "If angels were living on the earth, in peace and quiet, We would have sent to them an angel from heaven as a messenger."(17:95)

قُل لَّوۡ كَانَ فِى ٱلۡأَرۡضِ مَلَـٰٓئِكَةٌ يَمۡشُونَ مُطۡمَئِنِّينَ لَنَزَّلۡنَا عَلَيۡهِم مِّنَ ٱلسَّمَآءِ مَلَكًا رَسُولًا ۝

سورة الإسراء : ٩٥

For each (person), there are (angels) before and behind him who guard him by the command of God. Truly, God will never change the condition of a people until they change it themselves (with their own souls). Once God wills a people's punishment, it cannot be turned back, nor will they find any protector other than Him. (13:11)

لَهُۥ مُعَقِّبَـٰتٌ مِّنۢ بَيۡنِ يَدَيۡهِ وَمِنۡ خَلۡفِهِۦ يَحۡفَظُونَهُۥ مِنۡ أَمۡرِ ٱللَّهِ إِنَّ ٱللَّهَ لَا يُغَيِّرُ مَا بِقَوۡمٍ حَتَّىٰ يُغَيِّرُواْ مَا بِأَنفُسِهِمۡ وَإِذَآ أَرَادَ ٱللَّهُ بِقَوۡمٍ سُوٓءًا فَلَا مَرَدَّ لَهُۥ وَمَا لَهُم مِّن دُونِهِۦ مِن وَالٍ ۝

سورة الرعد : ١١

Truly (angles have been appointed) to protect you. (82:10)

وَإِنَّ عَلَيۡكُمۡ لَحَـٰفِظِينَ ۝   سورة الانفطار : ١٠

Each soul has a protector. (86:4)

إِن كُلُّ نَفۡسٍ لَّمَّا عَلَيۡهَا حَافِظٌ ۝   سورة الطارق : ٤

Or do they think that We do not hear their secrets and their private counsels? Truly (We do), and Our messengers are by them to record. (43:80)

أَمۡ يَحۡسَبُونَ أَنَّا لَا نَسۡمَعُ سِرَّهُمۡ وَنَجۡوَىٰهُم بَلَىٰ وَرُسُلُنَا لَدَيۡهِمۡ يَكۡتُبُونَ ۝

سورة الزخرف : ٨٠

Behold, two (guardian angels) appointed to learn (what he does) learn (and note them), one sitting on the right and one on the left. (50:17)

إِذۡ يَتَلَقَّى ٱلۡمُتَلَقِّيَانِ عَنِ ٱلۡيَمِينِ وَعَنِ ٱلشِّمَالِ قَعِيدٌ ۝

سورة ق : ١٧

They have been known to aid those fighting for right and actually appear in battle to frighten their enemies. They do not necessarily take part in the fighting (3:124-25; 8:9).

Remember that you said to the faithful, "Is it not enough for you that God helps you by sending three thousand angels? If you remain firm and act rightly, your Lord would help you with five thousand angels, who would make a terrific onslaught, if the enemy should attack you vigorously. (3:124-125)

إِذْ تَقُولُ لِلْمُؤْمِنِينَ أَلَن يَكْفِيَكُمْ أَن يُمِدَّكُمْ رَبُّكُم بِثَلَٰثَةِ ءَالَٰفٍ مِّنَ ٱلْمَلَٰٓئِكَةِ مُنزَلِينَ ۝ بَلَىٰ إِن تَصْبِرُوا۟ وَتَتَّقُوا۟ وَيَأْتُوكُم مِّن فَوْرِهِمْ هَٰذَا يُمْدِدْكُمْ رَبُّكُم بِخَمْسَةِ ءَالَٰفٍ مِّنَ ٱلْمَلَٰٓئِكَةِ مُسَوِّمِينَ ۝

سورة آل عمران: ١٢٤-١٢٥

Remember that you asked your Lord for help, and He replied, "I will help you with a thousand angels, (arranged) in ranks." (8:9)

إِذْ تَسْتَغِيثُونَ رَبَّكُمْ فَٱسْتَجَابَ لَكُمْ أَنِّي مُمِدُّكُم بِأَلْفٍ مِّنَ ٱلْمَلَٰٓئِكَةِ مُرْدِفِينَ ۝

سورة الأنفال: ٩

The Angels Of Mons, 1914

Recent battles are more readily appreciated than those of the past. During the First World War, the *London Evening News* (26 August 1914) reported the memorable—some would say miraculous—Battle of Mons. Despite being outnumbered three to one by the Germans and suffering heavy casualties, the British retreat was extremely successful. According to some reports, the "Angels of Mons" suddenly stood between the two forces, and the German army fell back in confusion. A British officer who survived said that a troop of angels stood between them and the Germans and terrified the latter's horses, which stampeded in all directions. According to German records, their men refused to charge a point where the British line was broken because of the presence of many troops. According to Allied records, there was not a single British soldier in the area. The event was commemorated by a waltz entitled "Angels of Mons." People consider such stories to be legends, but those who take part in war know how true it can be. Sometimes battles are won when they should have been lost, and sometimes lost when they should have been won.

Another important task entrusted to angels is to "collect our spirits and visit death on us" (16:28). In the afterlife, they will meet man (21:103) and

have the difficult task of initiating his punishment (8:50). Nineteen of them
(74:30) will be guarding the seven doors of hell (15:44).

(As for) those whose lives the
angels take while they are
doing wrong to their own
souls, they will (pretend) to
submit (and say), "We did not
know that we were doing
something evil." (The angels
will reply), "God knows
everything that you did."
(16:28)

ٱلَّذِينَ تَوَفَّنهُمُ ٱلْمَلَٰٓئِكَةُ ظَالِمِىٓ أَنفُسِهِمْ فَأَلْقَوُا
ٱلسَّلَمَ مَا كُنَّا نَعْمَلُ مِن سُوٓءٍ بَلَىٰٓ
إِنَّ ٱللَّهَ عَلِيمٌۢ بِمَا كُنتُمْ تَعْمَلُونَ ۝

سورة النحل: ٢٨

The Great Terror will cause
them no grief, for the angels
will meet them (and say),
"This is your day, (the one)
that was promised to you."
(21:103)

لَا يَحْزُنُهُمُ ٱلْفَزَعُ ٱلْأَكْبَرُ وَتَتَلَقَّىٰهُمُ
ٱلْمَلَٰٓئِكَةُ هَٰذَا يَوْمُكُمُ ٱلَّذِى
كُنتُمْ تُوعَدُونَ ۝

سورة الأنبياء: ١٠٣

If you could see the angels
when they take the souls of the
unbelievers (at death), (how)
they smite their faces and
backs (while saying), "Taste
the penalty of the blazing fire."
(8:50)

وَلَوْ تَرَىٰٓ إِذْ يَتَوَفَّى ٱلَّذِينَ كَفَرُوا ٱلْمَلَٰٓئِكَةُ
يَضْرِبُونَ وُجُوهَهُمْ وَأَدْبَٰرَهُمْ
وَذُوقُوا عَذَابَ ٱلْحَرِيقِ ۝

سورة الأنفال: ٥٠

Over it are nineteen (angels).
(74:30)

عَلَيْهَا تِسْعَةَ عَشَرَ ۝
سورة المدثر: ٣٠

(Hell) has seven gates, for each
gate has assigned to it a (special) class (of sinners). (15:44)

لَهَا سَبْعَةُ أَبْوَٰبٍ لِّكُلِّ بَابٍ مِّنْهُمْ
جُزْءٌ مَّقْسُومٌ ۝
سورة الحجر: ٤٤

Angels are obedient creatures that act only according to God's command. They pray to Him and worship Him continuously. When He asked
them to kneel to man (15:28-29), whom He had made out of mud, all but
Iblis obeyed (15:30-31). God asked the angels to kneel to man in recognition of the struggle that man would have to undertake to live according to
his virtuous (angelic) nature and not his bestial (animal) nature. Certainly,
those who win this inner battle and become more virtuous than bestial
deserve recognition by the angels themselves.

Your Lord said to the angels, "I am about to create man from clay, from mud that has been shaped. After I have fashioned him (in due proportion) and breathed into him of My spirit, prostrate in obedience to him." All of the angels did as they were told, except Iblīs, who refused to prostrate. (15:28-31)

وَإِذْ قَالَ رَبُّكَ لِلْمَلَـٰٓئِكَةِ إِنِّى خَـٰلِقٌۢ بَشَرًا مِّن صَلْصَـٰلٍ مِّنْ حَمَإٍ مَّسْنُونٍ ۝

فَإِذَا سَوَّيْتُهُۥ وَنَفَخْتُ فِيهِ مِن رُّوحِى فَقَعُوا۟ لَهُۥ سَـٰجِدِينَ ۝

فَسَجَدَ ٱلْمَلَـٰٓئِكَةُ كُلُّهُمْ أَجْمَعُونَ ۝

إِلَّآ إِبْلِيسَ أَبَىٰٓ أَن يَكُونَ مَعَ ٱلسَّـٰجِدِينَ ۝

سورة الحجر: ٢٨-٣١

The Modern Perception of Angels

At the present time, there are more reports than ever before of people seeing angels. In a national poll taken in the United States and published in *Time* magazine (1993), 69 percent of all Americans believe in angels, and 32 percent of those stated that they had had a personal encounter with angels. Moreover, there are now angel seminars, angel lectures, angel newsletters, and even people who can contact your personal guardian angel. In "Entertaining Angels Unawares," a program produced by ITV for Channel 3 (London) and broadcasted on 19 December 1995, 49 interviewees from England and the United States reported encounters with angels. It also showed a seminar held in London to help people meet their guardian angel. However, Dr. Peter Fenwick, (Consultant Neuropsychiatrist Maudsley Hospital, England) and Professor Bill Deakin (Professor of Psychiatry, Manchester Royal Infirmary) believe that seeing angels is an experience and function of the brain. In other words, it does not come from an external source. The television program wondered whether scientists were mistaken. While scientists can explain some angel experiences as related to brain function(s), their explanations do not always hold up, especially when a vision is reported by several unrelated people. The program closed by wondering whether angels are making themselves known to us, either visibly or invisibly, and whether we are indeed entertaining angels unawares.

The Devil

The Devil has many names: Iblīs, Shayṭān, Satan, and Wiswās (one who conducts a persistent malicious whispering in people's mind). As mentioned earlier, the Devil refused to obey God's command to kneel before the newly created man, for he felt it was not befitting for him to do so. After all, he was a jinn who had been made of fire (18:50) and therefore should not be required to kneel before a creature made of mud.

We said to the angels, "Bow down to Adam." They all did so, except Iblis, one of the jinn. He disobeyed his Lord. Will you take him and his progeny as your protectors rather than Me? They are your enemies! Such an exchange would be evil for those who do wrong. (18:50)

وَإِذْ قُلْنَا لِلْمَلَـٰٓئِكَةِ ٱسْجُدُوا۟ لِـَٔادَمَ فَسَجَدُوٓا۟
إِلَّآ إِبْلِيسَ كَانَ مِنَ ٱلْجِنِّ فَفَسَقَ عَنْ أَمْرِ رَبِّهِۦٓ
أَفَتَتَّخِذُونَهُۥ وَذُرِّيَّتَهُۥٓ أَوْلِيَآءَ مِن دُونِى
وَهُمْ لَكُمْ عَدُوٌّۢ بِئْسَ لِلظَّـٰلِمِينَ بَدَلًا ٥٠

سورة الكهف: ٥٠.

God cast the Devil out of heaven for being so vain and disobedient. The Devil, in turn, begged God to let him use all of his powers until the Day of Judgment in order to prove to God that man and his descendants could be led astray easily.

(God) said, "Get out of here. You are not to be arrogant here, for you come from the meanest (of creatures)." (Iblis) replied, "Allow me (to work) among them until You raise them up." (God) said, "I grant your request." (Iblis) said, "Because You have cast me off the straight path, I will lay in wait for them on Your straight path. I will attack them from the front and from the rear, form the right and from the left. You will find most of them ungrateful (for Your mercies)." (God) replied, "Get out of here, (for you have been) disgraced and expelled. If anyone should follow you, I will fill Hell with all of you." (7:13-18)

قَالَ فَٱهْبِطْ مِنْهَا فَمَا يَكُونُ لَكَ أَن تَتَكَبَّرَ
فِيهَا فَٱخْرُجْ إِنَّكَ مِنَ ٱلصَّـٰغِرِينَ ١٣
قَالَ أَنظِرْنِىٓ إِلَىٰ يَوْمِ يُبْعَثُونَ ١٤
قَالَ إِنَّكَ مِنَ ٱلْمُنظَرِينَ ١٥
قَالَ فَبِمَآ أَغْوَيْتَنِى لَأَقْعُدَنَّ لَهُمْ صِرَٰطَكَ ٱلْمُسْتَقِيمَ ١٦
ثُمَّ لَـَٔاتِيَنَّهُم مِّنۢ بَيْنِ أَيْدِيهِمْ وَمِنْ خَلْفِهِمْ وَعَنْ أَيْمَـٰنِهِمْ
وَعَن شَمَآئِلِهِمْ وَلَا تَجِدُ أَكْثَرَهُمْ شَـٰكِرِينَ ١٧
قَالَ ٱخْرُجْ مِنْهَا مَذْءُومًا مَّدْحُورًا لَّمَن تَبِعَكَ مِنْهُمْ
لَأَمْلَأَنَّ جَهَنَّمَ مِنكُمْ أَجْمَعِينَ ١٨

سورة الأعراف: ١٣-١٨

The Devil threatened to tempt human beings from the straight path through their life, children, money, and persuasion. When they disbelieve, he disclaims all responsibility (8:48). In front of God, he declares that he can not keep his promises to them and that they have only themselves to blame (14:22).

Remember that the Devil made their (sinful) acts seem alluring to them. He said, "No man can overcome you today while I am near you." But when the two forces came in sight of one another, He turned on his heels and said, "I am free of you, for I see what you do not. I fear God, for God is strict in punishment." (8:48)

وَإِذْ زَيَّنَ لَهُمُ ٱلشَّيْطَانُ أَعْمَالَهُمْ وَقَالَ لَا غَالِبَ لَكُمُ ٱلْيَوْمَ مِنَ ٱلنَّاسِ وَإِنِّي جَارٌ لَّكُمْ فَلَمَّا تَرَآءَتِ ٱلْفِئَتَانِ نَكَصَ عَلَىٰ عَقِبَيْهِ وَقَالَ إِنِّي بَرِىٓءٌ مِّنكُمْ إِنِّىٓ أَرَىٰ مَا لَا تَرَوْنَ إِنِّىٓ أَخَافُ ٱللَّهَ وَٱللَّهُ شَدِيدُ ٱلْعِقَابِ ۝

سورة الأنفال: ٤٨

Satan will say, when the matter is decided, "It was God Who gave you a true promise. I promised you, but I failed to carry it out. I only had authority to call you, and it was you who (agreed to) listen to me. Do not reproach me, but reproach your own souls. I cannot listen to your cries, and you cannot listen to mine. I reject your former act of associating me with God. For those who do wrong, there must be a grievous penalty." (14:22)

وَقَالَ ٱلشَّيْطَانُ لَمَّا قُضِىَ ٱلْأَمْرُ إِنَّ ٱللَّهَ وَعَدَكُمْ وَعْدَ ٱلْحَقِّ وَوَعَدتُّكُمْ فَأَخْلَفْتُكُمْ وَمَا كَانَ لِىَ عَلَيْكُم مِّن سُلْطَانٍ إِلَّآ أَن دَعَوْتُكُمْ فَٱسْتَجَبْتُمْ لِى فَلَا تَلُومُونِى وَلُومُوٓا أَنفُسَكُم مَّآ أَنَا۠ بِمُصْرِخِكُمْ وَمَآ أَنتُم بِمُصْرِخِىَّ إِنِّى كَفَرْتُ بِمَآ أَشْرَكْتُمُونِ مِن قَبْلُ إِنَّ ٱلظَّالِمِينَ لَهُمْ عَذَابٌ أَلِيمٌ ۝

سورة إبراهيم: ٢٢

It is not clear how the Devil affects man. One is aware of a psychological side of the human mind called the id, from the Greek word *idios* (peculiar). Freud used this term to describe man's self-preservative tendencies and instincts as a totality—the true unconscious. It is the reservoir of instinctive impulses and is dominated by the pleasure principle. The Devil seems to play an important role in influencing such instinctive impulses (114:4-5). It is a psychologically accepted phenomenon that remembering the name of God will cancel the Devil's influence (41:36). A person who intends to commit an evil act may be dissuaded from doing so by a virtuous idea, music, a picture of a friend, and so on. Remembering God has a spiritual, virtuous, and calming effect on many people.

From the mischief of the one who whispers (evil) and (then) withdraws, (the same one) who whispers in the hearts of men. (114:4-5)

مِن شَرِّ ٱلْوَسْوَاسِ ٱلْخَنَّاسِ ۝ ٱلَّذِى يُوَسْوِسُ فِى صُدُورِ ٱلنَّاسِ ۝

سورة الناس: ٤-٥

Say, "My God, I seek refuge
with You from the suggestions
of those who are evil." (23:97)

وَقُل رَّبِّ أَعُوذُ بِكَ مِنْ هَمَزَٰتِ ٱلشَّيَٰطِينِ ۝

سورة المؤمنون: ٩٧

If (at any time) you are incited
to discord by the Evil One, seek
refuge in God, Who knows and
hears everything. (41:36)

وَإِمَّا يَنزَغَنَّكَ مِنَ ٱلشَّيْطَٰنِ نَزْغٌ فَٱسْتَعِذْ بِٱللَّهِ
إِنَّهُۥ هُوَ ٱلسَّمِيعُ ٱلْعَلِيمُ ۝

سورة فصلت: ٣٦

When Adam and Eve were first created, they lived in the Garden of
Paradise and ate whatever they wished, except for the fruit of the forbidden
tree. The Devil, using all of his persuasive powers of evil, asserted that they
would become angels or immortal if they would eat that fruit. When they
took his advice and did as he wished, they were cast out of Paradise and
sent to live on Earth with an established enemy: the Devil and his assistants
(the jinn).

"O Adam. You and your wife
will dwell in the Garden and
enjoy (its good things) as you
wish. But do not approach this
tree, for (doing so) will result
in harm and transgression."
Then Satan began to whisper
suggestions to them so that
they would see their shame,
which previously had been
hidden from them. He said,
"Your Lord only forbade you
(to eat) from this tree lest you
become angels or immortal,"
and swore that he was their
sincere advisor. Thus, he
brought about their fall by
deceit, for when they tasted of
the tree, their shame became
visible to them and they began
to sew together the leaves of
the Garden (and place them)
over their bodies. And their
Lord called to them, "Did I not
forbid you (to eat from) that
tree and tell you that Satan
was your avowed enemy?"
(7:19-22)

وَيَٰٓـَٔادَمُ ٱسْكُنْ أَنتَ وَزَوْجُكَ ٱلْجَنَّةَ فَكُلَا مِنْ حَيْثُ
شِئْتُمَا وَلَا تَقْرَبَا هَٰذِهِ ٱلشَّجَرَةَ فَتَكُونَا مِنَ ٱلظَّٰلِمِينَ ۝
فَوَسْوَسَ لَهُمَا ٱلشَّيْطَٰنُ لِيُبْدِىَ لَهُمَا مَا وُۥرِىَ
عَنْهُمَا مِن سَوْءَٰتِهِمَا وَقَالَ مَا نَهَىٰكُمَا رَبُّكُمَا
عَنْ هَٰذِهِ ٱلشَّجَرَةِ إِلَّآ أَن تَكُونَا مَلَكَيْنِ أَوْ تَكُونَا
مِنَ ٱلْخَٰلِدِينَ ۝
وَقَاسَمَهُمَآ إِنِّى لَكُمَا لَمِنَ ٱلنَّٰصِحِينَ ۝
فَدَلَّىٰهُمَا بِغُرُورٍ فَلَمَّا ذَاقَا ٱلشَّجَرَةَ بَدَتْ لَهُمَا
سَوْءَٰتُهُمَا وَطَفِقَا يَخْصِفَانِ عَلَيْهِمَا مِن وَرَقِ ٱلْجَنَّةِ
وَنَادَىٰهُمَا رَبُّهُمَآ أَلَمْ أَنْهَكُمَا عَن تِلْكُمَا
ٱلشَّجَرَةِ وَأَقُل لَّكُمَآ إِنَّ ٱلشَّيْطَٰنَ لَكُمَا عَدُوٌّ مُّبِينٌ ۝

سورة الأعراف: ١٩-٢٢

Jinn (invisible beings)

The jinn were created before man from a type of smokeless fire called al Samūm.

We created man from sounding clay, from mud molded into shape. As for the jinn, we had created them before from the fire of a scorching wind. (15:26-27)	وَلَقَدْ خَلَقْنَا ٱلْإِنسَٰنَ مِن صَلْصَٰلٍ مِّنْ حَمَإٍ مَّسْنُونٍ ۝ وَٱلْجَآنَّ خَلَقْنَٰهُ مِن قَبْلُ مِن نَّارِ ٱلسَّمُومِ ۝ سورة الحجر: ٢٦-٢٧
He created the jinn from a fire without smoke. (55:15)	وَخَلَقَ ٱلْجَآنَّ مِن مَّارِجٍ مِّن نَّارٍ ۝ سورة الرحمن: ١٥

They seem to have unusual powers, as one offered to bring prophet Solomon the throne of the Queen of Sheba from Yemen to Jerusalem before he left his council. Solomon used to hold his council from morning until sunset. In other words, this jinn offered to carry the throne between these two cities in a short time, not unlike that taken by an airplane.

One of the jinns, a large and powerful one, said, "I will bring it to you before you end your council. Truly, I have the power to perform such an act and can be trusted." (27:39)	قَالَ عِفْرِيتٌ مِّنَ ٱلْجِنِّ أَنَا۠ ءَاتِيكَ بِهِۦ قَبْلَ أَن تَقُومَ مِن مَّقَامِكَ وَإِنِّي عَلَيْهِ لَقَوِيٌّ أَمِينٌ ۝ سورة النمل: ٣٩

The jinn attended Solomon's council, formed part of his army, acted as his builders and divers, and perhaps taught men some of their skills.

Solomon's troops were marshalled in front of him: jinns, men, and birds, all kept in order and arranged by rank. (27:17)	وَحُشِرَ لِسُلَيْمَٰنَ جُنُودُهُۥ مِنَ ٱلْجِنِّ وَٱلْإِنسِ وَٱلطَّيْرِ فَهُمْ يُوزَعُونَ ۝ سورة النمل: ١٧
(We also subjected) the evil ones, (including) every kind of builder and diver (to Solomon's power). (38:37)	وَٱلشَّيَٰطِينَ كُلَّ بَنَّآءٍ وَغَوَّاصٍ ۝ سورة ص: ٣٧

Some are good, whereas others are evil. The latter act as agents and comrades of Satan and are assigned to lead human beings astray.

Some of us submit our wills (to God) while others depart from justice. Those who submit their wills have sought out (the path) of right conduct, whereas those who have departed are fuel for the fires of Hell. (72:14-15)

وَأَنَّا مِنَّا ٱلْمُسْلِمُونَ وَمِنَّا ٱلْقَـٰسِطُونَ فَمَنْ أَسْلَمَ فَأُو۟لَـٰٓئِكَ تَحَرَّوْا۟ رَشَدًا ﴿١٤﴾ وَأَمَّا ٱلْقَـٰسِطُونَ فَكَانُوا۟ لِجَهَنَّمَ حَطَبًا ﴿١٥﴾

سورة الجن: ١٤-١٥

If anyone withdraws himself from the remembrance of (God) Most Gracious, We appoint an evil one to be his intimate companion. (43:36)

وَمَن يَعْشُ عَن ذِكْرِ ٱلرَّحْمَـٰنِ نُقَيِّضْ لَهُۥ شَيْطَـٰنًا فَهُوَ لَهُۥ قَرِينٌ ﴿٣٦﴾

سورة الزخرف: ٣٦

The jinn thought, wrongly, that they could escape God by flying about on Earth. They tried to listen to the high council of heaven, but were unable to do so, for God uses "strong guards and flames" to guard the lower heaven. Furthermore, those who tried to listen found "guided flame missiles" waiting for them.

But we think that we cannot frustrate God either upon the earth or by flight. (72:12)

وَأَنَّا ظَنَنَّآ أَن لَّن نُّعْجِزَ ٱللَّهَ فِى ٱلْأَرْضِ وَلَن نُّعْجِزَهُۥ هَرَبًا ﴿١٢﴾   سورة الجن: ١٢

We pried into the secrets of heaven and found it filled with stern guards and flaming fires. Truly, we used to sit there in (hidden) places to (eavesdrop) on what was being said. However, any who listens now will find a flaming fire waiting in ambush for him. (72:8-9)

وَأَنَّا لَمَسْنَا ٱلسَّمَآءَ فَوَجَدْنَـٰهَا مُلِئَتْ حَرَسًا شَدِيدًا وَشُهُبًا ﴿٨﴾ وَأَنَّا كُنَّا نَقْعُدُ مِنْهَا مَقَـٰعِدَ لِلسَّمْعِ فَمَن يَسْتَمِعِ ٱلْـَٔانَ يَجِدْ لَهُۥ شِهَابًا رَّصَدًا ﴿٩﴾

سورة الجن: ٨-٩

Supernatural Humans

God gave supernatural powers to almost all of his prophets. For example, He gave Prophet Muhammad the Qur'an, which is written in very high Arabic. The Arabs used to hold contests—always unsuccessful—to see if one of them could imitate a verse or two of the Qur'an. It is still an open challenge that no one has yet met.

Jesus was created when God blew from His spirit into his mother, the Virgin Mary (21:91). God gave him the powers to raise the dead, cure the leper, and bring to life birds made of mud (5:110).

(Remember) the woman who guarded her chastity. We breathed into her of Our Spirit and made her and her son a sign for all people. (21:91)

وَٱلَّتِىٓ أَحْصَنَتْ فَرْجَهَا فَنَفَخْنَا فِيهَا مِن رُّوحِنَا وَجَعَلْنَٰهَا وَٱبْنَهَآ ءَايَةً لِّلْعَٰلَمِينَ ۝

سورة الأنبياء: ٩١

Then God will say, "Jesus, son of Mary, recount My favor to you and your mother. Behold! I strengthened you with the holy spirit so you would speak to the people during your childhood and your maturity. I taught you the Book and Wisdom, the Torah and the Gospel. I allowed you to make a clay model of a bird, breathe into it, and bring it to life. I allowed you to heal those born blind and the lepers and to raise the dead. I also restrained the children of Israel from (harming) you when you showed them My clear signs and those who did not believe said, 'This is nothing but magic.'" (5:110)

إِذْ قَالَ ٱللَّهُ يَٰعِيسَى ٱبْنَ مَرْيَمَ ٱذْكُرْ نِعْمَتِى عَلَيْكَ وَعَلَىٰ وَٰلِدَتِكَ إِذْ أَيَّدتُّكَ بِرُوحِ ٱلْقُدُسِ تُكَلِّمُ ٱلنَّاسَ فِى ٱلْمَهْدِ وَكَهْلًا وَإِذْ عَلَّمْتُكَ ٱلْكِتَٰبَ وَٱلْحِكْمَةَ وَٱلتَّوْرَىٰةَ وَٱلْإِنجِيلَ وَإِذْ تَخْلُقُ مِنَ ٱلطِّينِ كَهَيْئَةِ ٱلطَّيْرِ بِإِذْنِى فَتَنفُخُ فِيهَا فَتَكُونُ طَيْرًا بِإِذْنِى وَتُبْرِئُ ٱلْأَكْمَهَ وَٱلْأَبْرَصَ بِإِذْنِى وَإِذْ تُخْرِجُ ٱلْمَوْتَىٰ بِإِذْنِى وَإِذْ كَفَفْتُ بَنِىٓ إِسْرَٰٓءِيلَ عَنكَ إِذْ جِئْتَهُم بِٱلْبَيِّنَٰتِ فَقَالَ ٱلَّذِينَ كَفَرُوا۟ مِنْهُمْ إِنْ هَٰذَآ إِلَّا سِحْرٌ مُّبِينٌ ۝

سورة المائدة: ١١٠

The Merciful and Knowledgeable Servant of God

Prophet Moses thought he was the most knowledgeable man of his time, for God had given him the power to perform many miracles. Eventually, he wished to meet someone more knowledgeable than himself. It was ordained that al Khiḍr, a merciful and knowledgeable servant of God, would meet Moses. When they met, Moses asked to join him and be educated during their journey. Al Khiḍr agreed on one condition: Moses would ask no questions until their answers were volunteered. When they got into a boat, al Khiḍr scuttled it. Moses said, "Good God! Do you want to drown us? This is unacceptable." Al Khiḍr said, "I told you not to question me." Moses apologized and promised to ask no more questions. They continued on their way until they found a boy, who al Khiḍr killed on the spot. Moses shouted, "You have killed an innocent youth who killed no one! This is unforgivable." Al Khiḍr said, "Did not I tell that you cannot have patience with me." Moses apologized and promised they would part company if he asked another question. After a long journey, they went into a village and were made to feel very unwelcome by its inhabitants. Al Khiḍr found a falling wall and rebuilt it. Moses said, "We could have made some money out of that." Al Khiḍr replied, "Now we will part, for you have broken your promise. How can you have patience when you do not have the knowledge?"

He continued, "Now I will explain the reasons behind my actions. I have only acted on God's command. The boat I sunk belonged to needy people. At that time, however, the king was confiscating all good boats. I therefore made it unseaworthy so the king's men would not take it. The boy was the son of religious parents but was destined to be blasphemous, rebellious, and cause them deep grief. God took him in order to exchange him for a better, affectionate, and purer youth. Beneath the falling wall was a buried treasure, to which two orphan boys were entitled. Their father had been a righteous man, and God wanted them to grow up and retrieve their own treasure."

They found one of our servants upon whom We had bestowed mercy and knowledge from Our Presence. Moses said to him, "Can I follow you and learn some of what you know?" (Al Khiḍr) said, "You do not have the patience for such an undertaking, for your understanding is incomplete." Moses said, "You will find me patient, if God wills, and I will not disobey you." The other said, "Alright, you can accompany me, but ask me no questions until I volunteer the information." They began traveling and eventually got into a boat. (Al Khiḍr) made a hole in it, and Moses asked him if he were trying to drown the passengers. (Al Khiḍr) replied, "I told you to ask no questions." Moses apologized. They continued on their way until they met a young man, whom (Al Khiḍr) killed. Moses objected, "Why did you kill an innocent

فَوَجَدَا عَبْدًا مِّنْ عِبَادِنَآ ءَاتَيْنَٰهُ رَحْمَةً
مِّنْ عِندِنَا وَعَلَّمْنَٰهُ مِن لَّدُنَّا عِلْمًا ٦٥
قَالَ لَهُۥ مُوسَىٰ هَلْ أَتَّبِعُكَ عَلَىٰٓ أَن تُعَلِّمَنِ
مِمَّا عُلِّمْتَ رُشْدًا ٦٦
قَالَ إِنَّكَ لَن تَسْتَطِيعَ مَعِيَ صَبْرًا ٦٧
وَكَيْفَ تَصْبِرُ عَلَىٰ مَا لَمْ تُحِطْ بِهِۦ خُبْرًا ٦٨
قَالَ سَتَجِدُنِي إِن شَآءَ ٱللَّهُ صَابِرًا
وَلَآ أَعْصِي لَكَ أَمْرًا ٦٩
قَالَ فَإِنِ ٱتَّبَعْتَنِي فَلَا تَسْـَٔلْنِي عَن شَىْءٍ
حَتَّىٰٓ أُحْدِثَ لَكَ مِنْهُ ذِكْرًا ٧٠
فَٱنطَلَقَا حَتَّىٰٓ إِذَا رَكِبَا فِي ٱلسَّفِينَةِ خَرَقَهَا قَالَ
أَخَرَقْتَهَا لِتُغْرِقَ أَهْلَهَا لَقَدْ جِئْتَ شَيْـًٔا إِمْرًا ٧١
قَالَ أَلَمْ أَقُلْ إِنَّكَ لَن تَسْتَطِيعَ مَعِيَ صَبْرًا ٧٢
قَالَ لَا تُؤَاخِذْنِي بِمَا نَسِيتُ وَلَا تُرْهِقْنِي
مِنْ أَمْرِي عُسْرًا ٧٣
فَٱنطَلَقَا حَتَّىٰٓ إِذَا لَقِيَا غُلَٰمًا فَقَتَلَهُۥ قَالَ أَقَتَلْتَ
نَفْسًا زَكِيَّةً بِغَيْرِ نَفْسٍ لَّقَدْ جِئْتَ شَيْـًٔا نُّكْرًا ٧٤

man who has killed no one. This is evil, indeed." (Al Khiḍr) replied, "I told you to ask no questions." Moses apologized and said that he would leave him if he questioned him again. They continued on their way. They reached a village and, seeking food, were refused all hospitality. (Al Khiḍr) saw a wall on the point of collapse and fixed it. Moses said, "You could have been paid for that work." Al Khiḍr said, "Now I will leave you, but first let me explain my actions. The boat that I damaged belonged to several poor men who used it for their livelihood. As there was a king who was seizing all boats by force, I made it unserviceable. As for the youth, he came from parents of faith. However, we knew he would grow up rebellious and full of ingratitude (to God), and so we desired that God would give his parents a youth pure (of conduct) and closer in affection. As for the wall, it belonged to two local orphans. Underneath it was a treasure that had been buried by their father, a righteous man, to which they were entitled. God, in His mercy, wanted them to find it when they had attained their age and full strength. I have acted only according to the will of God. Such is the interpretation of what was beyond your own understanding. (18:65-82)

قَالَ أَلَمْ أَقُل لَّكَ إِنَّكَ لَن تَسْتَطِيعَ مَعِيَ صَبْرًا ۝

قَالَ إِن سَأَلْتُكَ عَن شَيْءٍ بَعْدَهَا فَلَا تُصَٰحِبْنِي قَدْ بَلَغْتَ مِن لَّدُنِّي عُذْرًا ۝

فَٱنطَلَقَا حَتَّىٰٓ إِذَآ أَتَيَآ أَهْلَ قَرْيَةٍ ٱسْتَطْعَمَآ أَهْلَهَا فَأَبَوْا أَن يُضَيِّفُوهُمَا فَوَجَدَا فِيهَا جِدَارًا يُرِيدُ أَن يَنقَضَّ فَأَقَامَهُۥ قَالَ لَوْ شِئْتَ لَتَّخَذْتَ عَلَيْهِ أَجْرًا ۝

قَالَ هَٰذَا فِرَاقُ بَيْنِي وَبَيْنِكَ سَأُنَبِّئُكَ بِتَأْوِيلِ مَا لَمْ تَسْتَطِع عَّلَيْهِ صَبْرًا ۝

أَمَّا ٱلسَّفِينَةُ فَكَانَتْ لِمَسَٰكِينَ يَعْمَلُونَ فِي ٱلْبَحْرِ فَأَرَدتُّ أَنْ أَعِيبَهَا وَكَانَ وَرَآءَهُم مَّلِكٌ يَأْخُذُ كُلَّ سَفِينَةٍ غَصْبًا ۝

وَأَمَّا ٱلْغُلَٰمُ فَكَانَ أَبَوَاهُ مُؤْمِنَيْنِ فَخَشِينَآ أَن يُرْهِقَهُمَا طُغْيَٰنًا وَكُفْرًا ۝

فَأَرَدْنَآ أَن يُبْدِلَهُمَا رَبُّهُمَا خَيْرًا مِّنْهُ زَكَوٰةً وَأَقْرَبَ رُحْمًا ۝

وَأَمَّا ٱلْجِدَارُ فَكَانَ لِغُلَٰمَيْنِ يَتِيمَيْنِ فِي ٱلْمَدِينَةِ وَكَانَ تَحْتَهُۥ كَنزٌ لَّهُمَا وَكَانَ أَبُوهُمَا صَٰلِحًا فَأَرَادَ رَبُّكَ أَن يَبْلُغَآ أَشُدَّهُمَا وَيَسْتَخْرِجَا كَنزَهُمَا رَحْمَةً مِّن رَّبِّكَ وَمَا فَعَلْتُهُۥ عَنْ أَمْرِي ذَٰلِكَ تَأْوِيلُ مَا لَمْ تَسْطِع عَّلَيْهِ صَبْرًا ۝

سورة الكهف: ٦٥-٨٢

There is no scientific method that will prove the existence of supernatural creatures. However, for many years man has seen and observed phenomena beyond his understanding although he knew that something or someone must have caused them. Man's senses are limited and can be extended beyond their normal ability only with the aid of highly technical devices. For example, infra-red devices enhance night-time vision and ultra-sound can detect objects in the depths of the sea, in rocks, and in the human body. It is very unlikely, no matter how far science progresses, that one will ever be able to see angels or jinn. Furthermore, there are many creatures moving on the earth that, while undetectable by man, can be detected easily by animals.

Thus, man should not be surprised at his inability to see angels, jinn, or the Devil, all of whom are invisible to him. Their presence cannot be detected, as their communications are probably at a wavelength that cannot be perceived by man. It seems that Earth and its surrounding space is more crowded than we realize.

Science and Superstition

Many events befalling man cannot be explained scientifically. Lucky events are always taken light-heartedly and without a second thought. However, such unhappy events as psychological and mental disorders, are usually taken very seriously. In the Middle Ages, nuns and priests used to treat hysterical paralysis and aphonia by drowning and stoning, for they believed such disorders were caused by demonic possession. Similar practices were found everywhere in the world at that time. Even now the world still hears about different religious sects that offer sacrifices to exorcise demons. They go through so many rituals that cannot be accepted scientifically. People take their loved ones to non-medical therapists in the hope that their psychological or mental disorders will be cured. They go through a lot of trouble and, perhaps, rituals that cannot be accepted by science.

The aetiology of psychological and mental disorders is still in its early days. Most research funds are directed toward heart disorders and cancer. Some attempts have been made to cure sex offenders by operating on his or her brain. There is now ongoing research to support the presence in the brain of receptors related to such diseases as schizophrenia and mania. One would not be surprised if, in the future, researchers discovered brain receptors that could be blocked and thereby "cure" patients from psychological and mental disorders. Electroconvulsive Therapy (ECT) or electroshock therapy has been used for many years to the treat such disorders. This treatment, given under anaesthesia and with a muscle relaxant, involves passing an electrical current through one or both sides of the brain in order to induce alterations in its electrical activity. Strict guidelines for this therapy's use have been provided by England's Royal College of Psychiatrists. It is used to combat depression, depression with severe paranoid ideas, suicidal tendencies, mutism, severe post-natal depression, and similar states. It is also part of the treatment for mania patients that do not respond to neuroliptic drugs. Although ECT's exact mode of action is not known, it seems to change the biogenic amines.

Scientific research usually catches up with the health problems that cause human anxiety. Perhaps when enough funds are directed to this field we might discover some evidence of the supernatural's effect on man.

CHAPTER SIX

THE CREATION OF MAN

Man is the most wonderful creation that has ever been produced. There are many examples that can prove this assertion. For example, a comparison between the size of a kidney machine, used for dialysing patients with renal failure, and the size of a human kidney is quite revealing in this respect. Hip and knee prosthesis have a limited span of life, may become infected, and require refashioning after 5-15 years, depending on use. An athletic man can sprint at 25 mph, throw a ball at 100 mph, and jump over 7 feet. The tendons joining his bones can stand a stress of 8 tons per square inch, and his thigh bones can take a strain of half a ton per square inch while walking. During his lifetime, an average man walks 7,000 miles if he lives in a city and 28,000 if he lives in the country.

His self-tailored waterproof skin suit, approximately 20 square feet of skin, is covered with around 5 million hairs, each of which lasts about 3 years. Human skin contains 4 million receptors that enable an individual to feel, distinguish cold from hot, and experience comfort or pain. The human heart pumps 10 pints of blood every minute of one's life and three times as much during exercise. The human body contains almost 60,000 miles of arteries, veins, and capillaries that, if extended, would cover 1.5 acres of land. They do not open all at once, for that would cause all of the body's blood to drain into them and engender a state of shock. The human body contains 2.5 trillion oxygen-bearing red cells and 2.5 billion white cells, all of which form the main part of our immune system. During the average human lifespan, an person will breathe 500 million times. Water forms 60 percent of one's body weight, while his brain—the world's most complex computer and the item that distinguishes man from animals—consists of about 3 pounds of grey-white matter and billions of working components. In a split second, it can make thousands of interconnected communications.

In spite of all this, God said that the creation of man was much easier than the creation of the heavens and the earth.

The creation of the heavens
and the earth is a greater (matter) than the creation of man,
but most people do not understand. (40:57)

لَخَلْقُ ٱلسَّمَٰوَٰتِ وَٱلْأَرْضِ أَكْبَرُ مِنْ خَلْقِ
ٱلنَّاسِ وَلَٰكِنَّ أَكْثَرَ ٱلنَّاسِ لَا يَعْلَمُونَ ٥٧

سورة غافر: ٥٧

Man is far weaker in constitution than other creatures. He was made
from "clinging clay" or mud, after which God breathed His spirit into him
and created his faculties of hearing and sight as well as his heart. His
descendants were made from "a strain of mean water" deriving from mixed
liquids. This statement is now known to be true, for a man's semen is made
of a mixture of fluids from the testicle, epididymis, and prostate.

Ask their opinion. Are they the
more difficult to create, or are
the (other) beings that We have
created? We have made them
out of a sticky clay. (37:11)

فَٱسْتَفْتِهِمْ أَهُمْ أَشَدُّ خَلْقًا أَم مَّنْ خَلَقْنَا
إِنَّا خَلَقْنَٰهُم مِّن طِينٍ لَّازِبٍ ١١

سورة الصافات: ١١

He who created everything
made His creation most good.
He began the creation of man
with (nothing more than) clay
and made his descendants from
an extract of a fluid held in low
esteem. He fashioned man in
due proportion, breathed something of His spirit into him. He
gave you the faculties of hearing, sight, and feeling (and
understanding). But you remain
ungrateful. (32:7-9)

ٱلَّذِىٓ أَحْسَنَ كُلَّ شَىْءٍ خَلَقَهُۥ وَبَدَأَ خَلْقَ
ٱلْإِنسَٰنِ مِن طِينٍ ٧
ثُمَّ جَعَلَ نَسْلَهُۥ مِن سُلَٰلَةٍ مِّن مَّآءٍ مَّهِينٍ ٨
ثُمَّ سَوَّىٰهُ وَنَفَخَ فِيهِ مِن رُّوحِهِۦ وَجَعَلَ لَكُمُ
ٱلسَّمْعَ وَٱلْأَبْصَٰرَ وَٱلْأَفْـِٔدَةَ قَلِيلًا
مَّا تَشْكُرُونَ ٩

سورة السجدة: ٧-٩

We created man from a drop of
mingled sperm. In order to try
him, We have allowed him to
hear and see. (76:2)

إِنَّا خَلَقْنَا ٱلْإِنسَٰنَ مِن نُّطْفَةٍ أَمْشَاجٍ نَّبْتَلِيهِ فَجَعَلْنَٰهُ
سَمِيعًا بَصِيرًا ٢

سورة الإنسان: ٢

Development and Embryology

Man develops from a drop to an 'alaqah (often translated as "blood
clot"). In the Arabic dictionary Mukhtār al Ṣiḥāḥ , it is stated that 'alaqah
could have several meanings: heavy blood, a water leech that lives on
blood, and, if it contains a double "l", something hanging or suspended. A
pregnant woman is considered to be 'alaqat (40:67). It is used in the plural

'alaq (96:2) or as pairs (35:11) to indicate a woman who is pregnant with two or more fetuses at the same time.

It is God who created you from dust, then from a drop of sperm, and then from a leech-like clot. After that, He brings you (into the light) as a child, lets you (grow and) reach your age of full strength, then become old— although some of you die before (that)—and lets you reach the lifespan that He has determined for you, so that you might gain wisdom. (40:67)

هُوَ ٱلَّذِى خَلَقَكُم مِّن تُرَابٍ ثُمَّ مِن نُّطْفَةٍ ثُمَّ مِنْ عَلَقَةٍ ثُمَّ يُخْرِجُكُمْ طِفْلًا ثُمَّ لِتَبْلُغُوٓا۟ أَشُدَّكُمْ ثُمَّ لِتَكُونُوا۟ شُيُوخًا وَمِنكُم مَّن يُتَوَفَّىٰ مِن قَبْلُ وَلِتَبْلُغُوٓا۟ أَجَلًا مُّسَمًّى وَلَعَلَّكُمْ تَعْقِلُونَ ۝

سورة غافر : ٦٧

(He) created man from a clot of congealed blood. (96:2)

خَلَقَ ٱلْإِنسَٰنَ مِنْ عَلَقٍ ۝   سورة العلق : ٢

God created you from dust, then from a drop of sperm, and then made you into pairs. No woman conceives or gives birth without His knowledge. A man does not live a long life or lose part of it without God having first decreed it. Such is easy for God. (35:11)

وَٱللَّهُ خَلَقَكُم مِّن تُرَابٍ ثُمَّ مِن نُّطْفَةٍ ثُمَّ جَعَلَكُمْ أَزْوَٰجًا وَمَا تَحْمِلُ مِنْ أُنثَىٰ وَلَا تَضَعُ إِلَّا بِعِلْمِهِۦ وَمَا يُعَمَّرُ مِن مُّعَمَّرٍ وَلَا يُنقَصُ مِنْ عُمُرِهِۦٓ إِلَّا فِى كِتَٰبٍ إِنَّ ذَٰلِكَ عَلَى ٱللَّهِ يَسِيرٌ ۝

سورة فاطر : ١١

He created man in stages (71:14). The first stage is that of a drop, which is soon transformed into a "hanging object" or "heavy blood." This develops into a piece of "chewed flesh," which is at first unformed and formed later into a definite shape. God decrees what is to be created inside the womb. After a suitable period of gestation, a child is born. It will become an adult, perhaps die, or reach the "vilest state of life" and loose all its previous knowledge (a possible reference to a condition not unlike Alzheimer's disease).

For it is God who has created you in different stages. (71:14)

وَقَدْ خَلَقَكُمْ أَطْوَارًا ۝ سورة نوح : ١٤

O mankind! If you have doubts about the resurrection, (consider) that we created you from

يَٰٓأَيُّهَا ٱلنَّاسُ إِن كُنتُمْ فِى رَيْبٍ مِّنَ ٱلْبَعْثِ فَإِنَّا خَلَقْنَٰكُم مِّن تُرَابٍ ثُمَّ مِن نُّطْفَةٍ ثُمَّ مِنْ عَلَقَةٍ

dust, then from a drop of sperm, then from a leech-like clot, and then out of a partly formed piece of flesh in order to show you Our power. We cause whom We will to rest in the wombs for an appointed term and then bring you forth as babes, then (take care of you) so that you might reach your age of full strength. Some of you are called to die, and some are sent back to the feeblest old age so that they will know nothing after having known (much). In addition, you see that the earth is barren and lifeless. However, when We send rain to water it, it is stirred to life and puts forth every kind of beautiful growth in pairs. (22:5)

ثُمَّ مِن مُّضۡغَةٍ مُّخَلَّقَةٍ وَغَيۡرِ مُخَلَّقَةٍ لِّنُبَيِّنَ لَكُمۡ وَنُقِرُّ فِى ٱلۡأَرۡحَامِ مَا نَشَآءُ إِلَىٰٓ أَجَلٍ مُّسَمًّى ثُمَّ نُخۡرِجُكُمۡ طِفۡلًا ثُمَّ لِتَبۡلُغُوٓاْ أَشُدَّكُمۡ وَمِنكُم مَّن يُتَوَفَّىٰ وَمِنكُم مَّن يُرَدُّ إِلَىٰٓ أَرۡذَلِ ٱلۡعُمُرِ لِكَيۡلَا يَعۡلَمَ مِنۢ بَعۡدِ عِلۡمٍ شَيۡـًٔا وَتَرَى ٱلۡأَرۡضَ هَامِدَةً فَإِذَآ أَنزَلۡنَا عَلَيۡهَا ٱلۡمَآءَ ٱهۡتَزَّتۡ وَرَبَتۡ وَأَنۢبَتَتۡ مِن كُلِّ زَوۡجٍۭ بَهِيجٍ ۝

سورة الحج: ٥

Further details of human development inside the womb are given, such as the fact that the drop is placed in a secure receptacle where it will be transformed into a suspended object and then into chewed flesh. After this stage, bones will be formed and covered with flesh.

We created man from an extract (of clay) and placed him, as (a drop of sperm), in a firmly fixed place of rest. Then We made the sperm into a clot of congealed blood, then that clot into a (fetal) lump, then that lump into bones that we then clothed with flesh, and then developed out of that another creature. Blessed be God, the Best One to create. (23:12-14)

وَلَقَدۡ خَلَقۡنَا ٱلۡإِنسَٰنَ مِن سُلَٰلَةٍ مِّن طِينٍ ۝ ثُمَّ جَعَلۡنَٰهُ نُطۡفَةً فِى قَرَارٍ مَّكِينٍ ۝ ثُمَّ خَلَقۡنَا ٱلنُّطۡفَةَ عَلَقَةً فَخَلَقۡنَا ٱلۡعَلَقَةَ مُضۡغَةً فَخَلَقۡنَا ٱلۡمُضۡغَةَ عِظَٰمًا فَكَسَوۡنَا ٱلۡعِظَٰمَ لَحۡمًا ثُمَّ أَنشَأۡنَٰهُ خَلۡقًا ءَاخَرَ فَتَبَارَكَ ٱللَّهُ أَحۡسَنُ ٱلۡخَٰلِقِينَ ۝

سورة المؤمنون: ١٢-١٤

The fetus's creation is said to occur in "three darknesses." This may refer to the three fetal membranes covering the fetus during its development (the amnion, the chorion, and the decidua [fig. 19]) or to the fetal membranes as one chamber, the uterus as the second, and the abdominal cavity as the third. The first explanation is generally accepted (Al Bār 1986).

God created (all of) you from a single person and then created a mate of like nature. He sent down for you eight head of cattle in pairs. He forms you in three veils of darkness, one after the other, while you are in your mother's womb. Such is God, your Lord and Cherisher. To Him belongs (all) dominion, and there is no god but He. Why, then, do you turn away? (39:6)

خَلَقَكُم مِّن نَّفْسٍ وَٰحِدَةٍ ثُمَّ جَعَلَ مِنْهَا زَوْجَهَا وَأَنزَلَ لَكُم مِّنَ ٱلْأَنْعَٰمِ ثَمَٰنِيَةَ أَزْوَٰجٍ يَخْلُقُكُمْ فِى بُطُونِ أُمَّهَٰتِكُمْ خَلْقًا مِّنۢ بَعْدِ خَلْقٍ فِى ظُلُمَٰتٍ ثَلَٰثٍ ذَٰلِكُمُ ٱللَّهُ رَبُّكُمْ لَهُ ٱلْمُلْكُ لَآ إِلَٰهَ إِلَّا هُوَ فَأَنَّىٰ تُصْرَفُونَ ۝

سورة الزمر : ٦

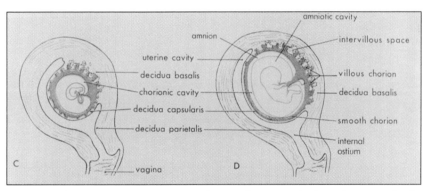

Figure 19: *This shows the three fetal membranes that cover the fetus during its development. It includes the amnion, the chorion, and the decidua.*

To summarize, the fetus's development starts with a "drop of mean water" formed of "mixed fluids" and placed in a "deep secure place." It is then developed in a "suspended stage" resembling "heavy blood," at which stage it will look like "chewed flesh" and bones will begin to form (at first the fetus will be unformed, but at a certain stage it will become formed). The human baby is not differentiated into a male or a female until it reaches full term. A modern embryologist could not have described this process of fetal development any better to a lay person fourteen centuries ago.

When a drop of a man's semen is introduced into a woman's vagina, millions of sperms are released. Only one needs to succeed in traveling the vast distance—roughly equivalent to a man going to the moon —between the cervix and the fallopian tube to fertilize the ovum. From the vagina, the sperm travels up the cervical canal and the uterine cavity along the fallopian tube, where it will find the ovum emerging from the ovary. The ovum, which has been taken up by the fimbria of the fallopian tube, will make its way toward the uterus. Fertilization, which takes place in the fallopian tube, will then produce the zygot that, in turn, will divide into cells. These cells then travel for approximately four to five days, at which time the blastocyst becomes free in the uterine cavity (fig. 20). Implantation of the blastocyst begins at the end of the first week of pregnancy (fig. 21) and is completed by the end of the second week.

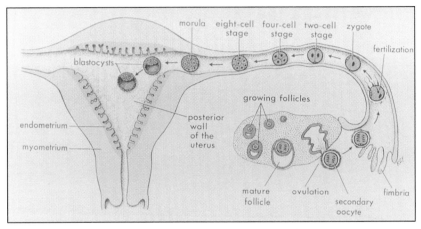

Figure 20. Diagram of the ovarian cycle, fertilization, and human development during the first 7 days.

If one could look inside the womb at this stage, he would see the human embryo hanging out or suspended as a protrusion from the womb's inner wall. This is called the endometrium (fig. 22), and is probably what is referred to as 'alaqah. The blastocyst's ('alaqah) outer layer, which is embedded in the uterus, is formed of syncytia (cytoplasm with multiple nuclei [i.e., many cells but with no cell wall]). Spaces, called lacunae, start to appear in this area (fig. 23), which will be opened and filled with maternal blood. The whole area represents the beginning of the placental circulation and is a very important developmental stage: 50 percent of the the fetus's genes are from the father and, strictly speaking, it is like a homography in the uterus that should be rejected by the mother. But this never happens. One explanation is that the area of the syncytia has no transplant antigen that could cause the

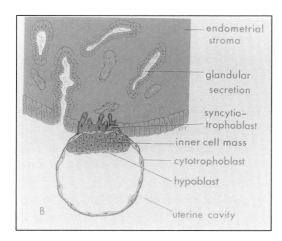

Figure 21: Diagram of the blastocyst at 7 days. The syncytiotrophoblast has started to penetrate the endometrium, which is the womb's inner layer. Note that the syncytia have no cell wall.

Figure 22: Photograph showing the endometrium, the womb's inner surface, with the human embryo implanted in it at approximately 12 days. (From Hertig AT, Rock J.: Contr Embryol Carneg Instn 29:127,1941).

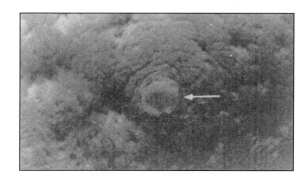

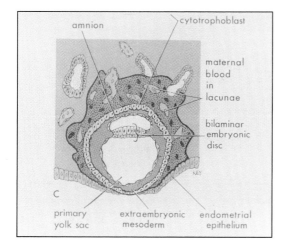

Figure 23: A sectional drawing of the blastocyst on about the ninth day when it is implanted in the endometrium. Note that the lacunae will be full of blood and will become the future placenta.

fetus to be rejected. Whatever the cause, this is a very important stage that protects the fetus.

What would it look like? It would be bloody and clingy. This is what 'alaqah looks like.

Early in the third week of pregnancy, the notochord is formed. This structure, which defines the primitive axis of the embryo, gives it some rigidity and indicates the future site of the vertebral column around which the axial skeleton will form (fig. 24). This shows beyond any doubt that the bones and the skeleton are the first elements to appear in the differentiation of man's creation, exactly as mentioned in the previous verse.

From the fourth to the eighth week of pregnancy, human development may be divided into three essential phases. The first is growth (increase in size), which involves cell division and the elaboration of cell products, or, in other words, chewed up flesh having no form or shape. The second process is morphogenesis (development of form). Again, exactly as mentioned in the previous verses, the formation of shape follows unformed flesh. The third phase is differentiation, at which time the maturation of physiological processes takes place. Figure 25 shows the embryo in the fourth week, figure 26 shows a human embryo at the age of fifty-one days, and figure 27 illustrates the shapes of the fetus from the ninth to the thirty-eighth week.

God was very precise in describing how the fetus is developed, for who can describe man better than the One who created him?

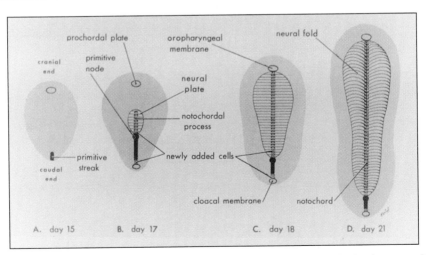

Figure 24: *An illustration of the notochord, which represents the early development of human bone. It starts on the fifteenth day and becomes well-recognized by the twenty-first.*

Figure 25: Photograph of the
embryo in the fourth week
before the fetus becomes fully
formed.

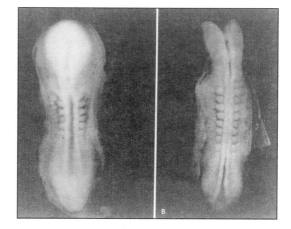

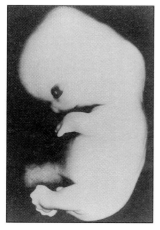

Figure 26: Photograph of an
almost fully-human embryo at
about 51 days.

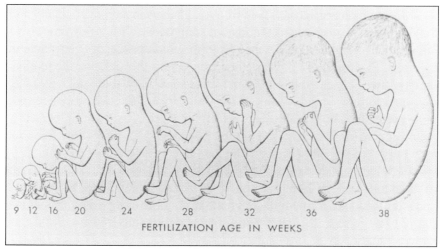

Figure 27: A drawing of the fetus from the ninth to the thirty-eighth week of pregnancy.
Hair starts to appear at about 20 weeks, and the eyes are open at about 26 weeks. The
scale of the drawing is about one-fifth actual size.

The Imager

God says that He images man inside the womb as He wishes and can compose him in any image He wishes. He is so proud of this fact that one of the names He has given Himself is "the Imager."

He is the one who shapes you in the wombs as He pleases. There is no god but Him, the Exalted in Might, the Wise. (3:6)

هُوَ ٱلَّذِى يُصَوِّرُكُمْ فِى ٱلْأَرْحَامِ كَيْفَ يَشَآءُ
لَآ إِلَٰهَ إِلَّا هُوَ ٱلْعَزِيزُ ٱلْحَكِيمُ ٦
سورة آل عمران: ٦

He Who created you, fashioned you in due proportion and made you symmetrical. He fashions you into whatever form He pleases. (82:7-8)

ٱلَّذِى خَلَقَكَ فَسَوَّىٰكَ فَعَدَلَكَ ٧
فِىٓ أَىِّ صُورَةٍ مَّا شَآءَ رَكَّبَكَ ٨
سورة الانفطار: ٧-٨

He is God, the Creator, the Evolver, the Bestower of Forms (or colors). To Him belong the most beautiful names. All that is in the heavens and on the Earth praises and glorifies Him. He is the Exalted in Might, the Wise. (59:24)

هُوَ ٱللَّهُ ٱلْخَٰلِقُ ٱلْبَارِئُ ٱلْمُصَوِّرُ لَهُ ٱلْأَسْمَآءُ
ٱلْحُسْنَىٰ يُسَبِّحُ لَهُ مَا فِى ٱلسَّمَٰوَٰتِ وَٱلْأَرْضِ
وَهُوَ ٱلْعَزِيزُ ٱلْحَكِيمُ ٢٤
سورة الحشر: ٢٤

Most human organs are made from two halves that unite gradually and longitudinally in the center. Anomalies may occur during this process of union, such as children born with a hare lip, a cleft palate, or even a hole in the heart. Figures 28-32 illustrate one example of this process: the gradual union of two separate tubes, each pulsating separately, that gradually unite to form a complete human heart. If the wall between the two tubes does not unite perfectly, a hole in the heart is formed. At twenty days of pregnancy, the heart consists of two pulsating tubes. At twenty-four days they fuse, but only during the eighth week is the human heart recognizable as such.

Each half of the heart is a mirror image of the other half, and each half of the human being is almost a mirror of the other half. Thus, a right hand and a left hand are formed: the left hand is a mirror of the right. If imaging did not take place, the appearance of two right hands and two right feet would result in severe problems.

How does God accomplish this imaging in the womb's darkness? He says that He created man from water and, although the proportion is the same in everyone, could vary them by gender, shape, size, color, and so on.

It is God who created man from water and then established relationships of lineage and marriage, for He has power (over all things). (25:54)

وَهُوَ ٱلَّذِى خَلَقَ مِنَ ٱلْمَآءِ بَشَرًا فَجَعَلَهُۥ نَسَبًا وَصِهْرًا وَكَانَ رَبُّكَ قَدِيرًا ﴿٥٤﴾

سورة الفرقان: ٥٤

Sixty percent of the body's weight is water. The remaining portion contains water molecules in its chemical structure. If one lost 10 percent of this water, he would be very ill. If 20 percent were lost, he would certainly die.

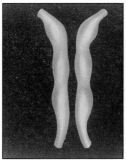

Figure 28

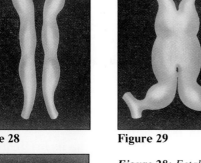

Figure 29

Figure 30

Figure 28: Fetal heart at 20 days: two pulsating tubes.

Figure 29: Fetal heart at 24 days: the two tubes fuse.

Figure 30: Fetal heart at 6 weeks: the tubes begin to twist around each other.

Figure 31: Fetal heart at 8 weeks: the unified tube has almost assumed the shape of a human heart.

Figure 32: Fetal heart later recognizable as a human heart.

Figure 31

Figure 32

Imaging, Genetic Coding, and DNA Fingerprints

God named Himself "The Imager," for, as He has said, He images us inside the womb in "three darknesses." It is extremely difficult to imagine how one is created in the dark, especially if one half of our body is to be the mirror image of the other half. A theory has been introduced recently that may help explain this unusual phenomenon of creation: Magnetic Resonance Imaging (MRI). This is a method of producing pictures in the X-ray department and may provide a partial explanation of what might happen during the process of embryonic development in the womb. The process may even be more complex in the case of twins, triplets, and other instances of multiple births at the same time.

Magnetic resonance produces images by using the magnetic properties of different tissues when placed within a magnetic field. Hydrogen, which is part of water, occurs in all tissues and is the most abundant element in the human body. Thus, its protons are used as MRI's signal source. If a human being is placed within a uniform magnetic field, these protons will align in the field's direction. If a radio frequency pulse is applied with a known frequency, the proton will resonate. When the radio frequency pulse stops, the proton will relax and resume its original position in the magnetic field. This relaxation time varies from tissue to tissue according to the hydrogen or water content. During this time, the proton releases its energy as a pulsed signal, and it is this signal that is used to create an MRI image. As different tissues produce different signal intensities, tissue can be demarcated on the image. Once the normal tissues are identified, diseased internal organs can be imaged without having to open the body (J. E. Husband 1991).

This may be one of many mechanisms God uses to image us inside the womb as a creation with one half being a mirror of the other.

The most outstanding discovery is that God creates a genetic map for each human being in the first cell created for each individual. This map will tell whether the person is going to be tall or short, dark or light, the color of his or her eyes, and so on.

Deoxyribonucleic Acid (DNA) and the Genetic Code

Scientists now know that DNA is a giant molecule containing, in a chemically coded form, all of the information needed to build, control, and maintain a living organism. It is a ladderlike double-stranded nucleic acid that forms the basis of genetic inheritance in all organisms, except for a few viruses that have only RNA. In non-bacteria organisms, it is organized into chromosomes and contained in the cell's nucleus. It is made up of two other chains of nucleotide subunits, each of which contains either a purine (adenine or guanine) or a pyrimidine (cytosine or thymine) base. The bases link up with each other, the adenine with the thymine and the cytosine with the guanine, to form the base pairs that connect the two strands of the DNA molecule like the rungs of a twisted ladder. The specific way in which the pairs form means that the base sequence is preserved from generation to generation. As a result, hereditary information is stored as a specific sequence of bases.

A set of three bases, known as a codon, acts as a blueprint for the manufacture of a particular amino acid, which is the subunit of a protein molecule. Codons are identified by the initial letters of their constituent bases. For example, the base sequence of codon CAG is cystosine-adenine-aguanine. The meaning of each codon in the genetic code has been worked out by molecular geneticists. There are four different bases, which means there must be 4 x 4 x 4 = 64 different codons. Proteins usually consist of only twenty different amino acids, so many amino acids have more than one codon: GGT, GGC, GGA and GGG are all codes for the same amino acid glycine. The data encoded by codons is transcribed by messenger RNA and is then translated into amino acids located in the ribosomes and cytoplasm.

The sequence of codons determines the precise order in which amino acids are linked during manufacture and the kind of protein to be produced. As proteins are the chief structural molecules of living matter and, as enzymes, regulate all aspects of metabolism, it may be said that the genetic code is responsible for building and controlling the entire organism. The sequence of bases along the length of the DNA molecule can be determined by cutting the molecule into small protons via restriction enzymes. This technique can also be used to transfer specific DNA sequences from one organism to another. In this way, the instructions for building proteins (the basic structural molecules of living matter) are "written" in the DNA's genetic material and are the basis of heredity. As a result, during development, each cell of the human body contains a blueprint for the rest of the body.

Genetic Fingerprinting or Genetic Profiling

God has made each individual in such a way that this technique can determine the pattern of certain parts of the DNA genetic material that is unique to each individual. Like fingerprinting, it can distinguish accurately between one individual and another, with the exception of identical siblings from multiple births, and can be applied to as little material as a single cell. It is performed by isolating the DNA and then comparing and contrasting its component chemical sequences with those of another individual(s). Any DNA pattern can be ascertained from a sample of skin, hair, or semen. Although differences are minimal (only .1 percent between unrelated people), certain regions of DNA, known as hypervariable regions, are unique. It is now allowed as a method of legal identification in such cases as paternity testing and forensic medicine, among others.

Recently, a new method has been introduced that makes it possible to represent the individual's genetic information in digital code. This development will make genetic fingerprinting more accurate than before. In 1993, a positive identification was made on the remains of an American soldier who had died in Vietnam twenty-nine years earlier. Subsequently, the United States Department of Defense launched a screening program to track tissue samples from military personnel for possible use in later identification.

This is a brief survey of how scientists view the imaging of a human embryo inside the womb; the complex genetic development that results in the structuring of our organs, heart, brain, our ability to hear and so on; and the genetic coding that, while different for every human being, is identical for every cell in each human being. Given this, it is not surprising that God calls Himself "the Imager."

The Sensory Infirm

God brings man into the world as a being without knowledge. He created his hearing, sight, and heart to help him during this life.

It is God Who brought you forth from your mothers' wombs when you knew nothing, and He allowed you to hear and see, and gave you intelligence and affection, so that you might give thanks (to Him). (16:78)

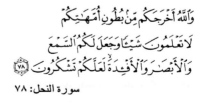

وَٱللَّهُ أَخْرَجَكُم مِّنۢ بُطُونِ أُمَّهَٰتِكُمْ لَا تَعْلَمُونَ شَيْئًا وَجَعَلَ لَكُمُ ٱلسَّمْعَ وَٱلْأَبْصَٰرَ وَٱلْأَفْـِٔدَةَ لَعَلَّكُمْ تَشْكُرُونَ ۝

سورة النحل: ٧٨

God has emphasized repeatedly that He created these three things. Without hearing and sight, a human being would be sensory infirm and unable to gain knowledge. Without the heart there would be no life. One can educate a human being if he has sight and no hearing and vice versa, but the absence of both faculties from birth would make this task very hard, if not impossible. Most health authorities do not have the skills and resources to nurse or care for those who are born sensory infirm, and nurses in this profession are highly skilled and confronted with many difficulties. This is why there are only a few specialized centers for the care of such individuals. The human heart is the gift of life and will be discussed after discussing how God created the first man.

Rūḥ: Spirit or Energy

As mentioned earlier, the first man (Adam) was created from mud or clay and then shaped by God, who breathed into him His *rūḥ* (spirit) (32:9). The *rūḥ* of God is the source of the difference between mud and a human being and is responsible for the production of a creature possessed of amazing energy and unlimited power. It seems that this energy did not stop at Adam, but that it is present in every human being, albeit in different concentrations in different parts of the body. This is what makes man different from other creatures.

This energy seems to have existed in minute units corresponding to each member of the human race. God took from the "backs of the children of Adam" their seed and asked them to testify on themselves that "He is their God." This implies that the energy put into Adam by God has been in every person since the very beginning of creation. It seems that it was also labeled for each person. The meaning of this verse goes beyond any imagination.

He fashioned man in due proportion, breathed something of His spirit into him, and gave him the faculties of hearing, sight, and feeling (and understanding). But you remain ungrateful. (32:9)

ثُمَّ سَوَّىٰهُ وَنَفَخَ فِيهِ مِن رُّوحِهِۦ وَجَعَلَ لَكُمُ ٱلسَّمْعَ وَٱلْأَبْصَٰرَ وَٱلْأَفْئِدَةَ قَلِيلًا مَّا تَشْكُرُونَ ۝

سورة السجدة: ٩

When God drew forth the descendants of the Children of Adam from their loins and made them testify concerning themselves, "Yes, we do testify," lest you should say on the Day of Judgment, "Truly we were not aware of this." (7:172)

وَإِذْ أَخَذَ رَبُّكَ مِنۢ بَنِىٓ ءَادَمَ مِن ظُهُورِهِمْ ذُرِّيَّتَهُمْ وَأَشْهَدَهُمْ عَلَىٰٓ أَنفُسِهِمْ أَلَسْتُ بِرَبِّكُمْ قَالُوا۟ بَلَىٰ شَهِدْنَآ أَن تَقُولُوا۟ يَوْمَ ٱلْقِيَٰمَةِ إِنَّا كُنَّا عَنْ هَٰذَا غَٰفِلِينَ ۝

سورة الأعراف: ١٧٢

Many questions have been asked about the *rūḥ*. God said that it is from His command. However, man was not given enough scientific knowledge to appreciate its nature.

They ask you of the spirit (of inspiration). Say, "The Spirit (comes) by the command of my Lord. Only a little knowledge has been given to you (O men)." (17:85)	وَيَسْأَلُونَكَ عَنِ ٱلرُّوحِ قُلِ ٱلرُّوحُ مِنْ أَمْرِ رَبِّي وَمَآ أُوتِيتُم مِّنَ ٱلْعِلْمِ إِلَّا قَلِيلًا ﴿٨٥﴾ سورة الإسراء: ٨٥

The *rūḥ* is never going to be understood. However, the electric potential of the heart, the brain, and other organs can be demonstrated. The *rūḥ* is the difference between mud and man, life and death. One of the strongest proofs of life is the heart, for it can be transplanted due to its ability to pulsate for several hours, given the right nutrients, temperature, and so on, without losing its viability. The heart's pulse is initiated spontaneously.

The human body is run by electricity. The biological electric potential created in the human body originates from its semipermeable membrane (it is partially permeable to potassium [K+] and sodium [NA+]). As a result of this membrane's electrical properties, a potential of approximately 0.1 volt is generated across the membrane. Changes in potentials of this type are the origin of such signals as the Electrocardiogram (ECG), the Electroencephalogram (EEG), and the Electromyogram (EMG).

Potassium ions are present inside the cells at a higher level of concentration than sodium ions, which causes a nerve fiber to have a potential of about -100 microvolts. The nerve is said to be polarized if it is excited by the flow of ionic current or by an external stimulus. The membrane character then changes, for sodium ions enter the cell and potassium ions leave it like an avalanche. This process is known as depolarization and initiates the nerve action's potential, which is then followed by a reversal: sodium ions depart and potassium ions enter the cell. This is how impulses travel along a nerve.

Nerve fibers are immersed in conducting fluids. Ionic currents flow around them from the polarized to the depolarized parts. These external currents are very important, for they are the only external evidence that an action potential is present and they engender most of the recordable bioelectric signals. For example, the heart gives rise to external currents of approximately 1 microamp when it is active. It is these currents that are detected by an ECG.

Bioelectric signals from the brain and an EEG are very difficult to record, for they are quite small—they have an amplitude of between 10 and 300 microvolts and a frequency content between 0.5 and 40 Hz. This is perhaps why they were not recorded until 1929 (the larger bioelectric signals of the heart were first recorded in 1895).

The Heart

The heart is the most important organ in the body, for it initiates the first electric signals. It has three points: the sino-atrial node (SA), the atrio-ventricular node (AV), and the His-Purkinje cells. The initiation of the heart's electrical activity is not produced by nervous stimulation but by specialized cells, known as pace-maker cells, in the three sites. In other words, such cells can initiate the pulse spontaneously and without help from other tissue, body chemicals, hormones, and so on. This property is called automaticity (i.e., automatic and perpetual). The SA node rate is 70-80 pulse/minute, the AV node is 40-50 pulse/minute, and the His-Purkinje cells rate is 30-40 pulse/minute. The normal resting potential of the SA node cell is about -90 microvolts (fig. 33). It changes slowly due to the steadily decreasing permeability of the cell membrane to potassium ions. Potassium ions are pumped into the cell, an inflow that is usually balanced by a passive leakage of potassium ions. If this linkage is reduced, the inside of the cell will become more positive. When the transmembrane potential reaches -75 microvolts, the membrane becomes permeable to sodium irons, which pass rapidly into the cell and result in its rapid depolarization. This is followed almost immediately by a rapid repolarization.

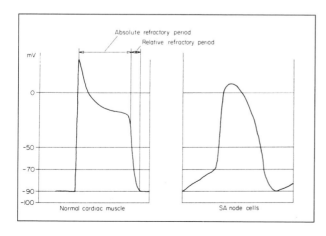

Figure 33: An intracellular electrical recording from an ordinary cardiac muscle cell and a sino-atrial mode cell.

The heart is the only organ having this property of automaticity. Once begun, these impulses spread throughout the rest of the heart muscle and then to the rest of the body. The electricity begun by the heart, which an ECG can measure, disappears when a person dies and cannot be detected by an ECG. There is no proof that the pulse-initiating cells could exist anywhere else in the body. The electricity is approximately 1 micronamp.

Any organ of the body may be propagated in a tissue culture, kept alive, and even multiply in a test tube for a variable period of time. The younger the person, the easier it is to propagate his tissue cells. This may mean that the energy present in the cells wanes as it grows older.

The Brain

God has many things to say about the brain. He always mentions the wonders of His creation, sets them as an example of His power, and asks people to examine the facts surrounding them with their brain. The verb used in these instances is *ya'qilūn*: to think with their brain. In one verse, He presents the creation of the heavens and the earth, the alternation of day and night, the sailing of ships in the sea, the rain that gives life to the dead earth, the spreading of animals on the planet, the control of wind and clouds between heaven and earth as signs for thinking people to appreciate His power and to realize His existence.

The brain is what differentiates man from animal. It is more complex than any man-made computer. Despite his present impressive and advanced scientific techniques, man is still unable to explore all of the brain's functions. As a result, many of its areas remain obscure.

Behold! In the creation of the heavens and the earth, in the alternation of night and day, in the sailing of ships through the ocean for the profit of mankind, in the rain that God sends from the skies and the life that He gives thereby to a dead earth, in the beasts of all kinds that He scatters throughout the earth, in the change of the winds and the clouds that trail them like slaves between the sky and the earth—(Here) indeed are signs for people who are wise (*ya'qilūn*). (2:164)

إِنَّ فِى خَلْقِ ٱلسَّمَٰوَٰتِ وَٱلْأَرْضِ وَٱخْتِلَٰفِ
ٱلَّيْلِ وَٱلنَّهَارِ وَٱلْفُلْكِ ٱلَّتِى تَجْرِى فِى ٱلْبَحْرِ
بِمَا يَنفَعُ ٱلنَّاسَ وَمَا أَنزَلَ ٱللَّهُ مِنَ ٱلسَّمَآءِ مِن مَّآءٍ
فَأَحْيَا بِهِ ٱلْأَرْضَ بَعْدَ مَوْتِهَا وَبَثَّ فِيهَا مِن
كُلِّ دَآبَّةٍ وَتَصْرِيفِ ٱلرِّيَٰحِ وَٱلسَّحَابِ
ٱلْمُسَخَّرِ بَيْنَ ٱلسَّمَآءِ وَٱلْأَرْضِ لَأَيَٰتٍ
لِّقَوْمٍ يَعْقِلُونَ ﴿١٦٤﴾

سورة البقرة: ١٦٤

Life Expectancy

The average life expectancy in the United Kingdom is about 72.4 years for men and 78.1 years for women. On the other hand, God tells us that Noah lived for 950 years. This might have been a special gift of God to Noah. However, it may also suggest that life expectancy has become shorter as the human race has progressed.

We sent Noah to his people, and he remained among them for nine hundred fifty years, but the Flood overwhelmed them while they (persisted in) sin. (29:14)	وَلَقَدْ أَرْسَلْنَا نُوحًا إِلَىٰ قَوْمِهِ، فَلَبِثَ فِيهِمْ أَلْفَ سَنَةٍ إِلَّا خَمْسِينَ عَامًا فَأَخَذَهُمُ ٱلطُّوفَانُ وَهُمْ ظَٰلِمُونَ ﴿١٤﴾ سورة العنكبوت: ١٤

Science and Angels

There are many words in the Qur'an that carry strong scientific meanings, but for some reason they were all given the same meaning: angels. Perhaps anything that looked or sounded supernatural had to be done by a supernatural creature.

The Immune System, Brain Receptors, and Printouts

God has placed *mu'aqqibbāt* between an individual's hands and behind him to protect him according to the will of God. The word *mu'aqibbāt* is explained as "angels attending to man." God may well have meant that He created our complex immune system to protect individuals from what He has already created around or inside them. However, he mentioned that every soul has a guardian angel or watcher who is a "noble writer" fully aware of what man does, plans, and conceals.

For each (person) there are (angels) before and behind him, guarding him by the command of God. Truly, God will never change the condition of a people until they change it themselves (with their own souls). Once God has willed a person's punishment, there is no turning it back, and neither will they find a protector other than Him. (13:11)	لَهُۥ مُعَقِّبَٰتٌ مِّنۢ بَيْنِ يَدَيْهِ وَمِنْ خَلْفِهِۦ يَحْفَظُونَهُۥ مِنْ أَمْرِ ٱللَّهِ إِنَّ ٱللَّهَ لَا يُغَيِّرُ مَا بِقَوْمٍ حَتَّىٰ يُغَيِّرُوا۟ مَا بِأَنفُسِهِمْ وَإِذَآ أَرَادَ ٱللَّهُ بِقَوْمٍ سُوٓءًا فَلَا مَرَدَّ لَهُۥ وَمَا لَهُم مِّن دُونِهِۦ مِن وَالٍ ﴿١١﴾ سورة الرعد: ١١

Every soul has a protector over it. (86:4)

إِن كُلُّ نَفْسٍ لَّمَّا عَلَيْهَا حَافِظٌ ۝

سورة الطارق: ٤

He is Irresistible, (watching) over His worshippers. He has set guardians over you. When death approaches one of you, Our angels take his soul and never fail in their duty. (6:61)

وَهُوَ ٱلْقَاهِرُ فَوْقَ عِبَادِهِۦ وَيُرْسِلُ عَلَيْكُمْ حَفَظَةً حَتَّىٰٓ إِذَا جَآءَ أَحَدَكُمُ ٱلْمَوْتُ تَوَفَّتْهُ رُسُلُنَا وَهُمْ لَا يُفَرِّطُونَ ۝

سورة الأنعام: ٦١

(Angels are appointed) over you to protect you. They are kind and honorable and write down (your deeds). They know and understand all that you do. (82:10-12)

وَإِنَّ عَلَيْكُمْ لَحَٰفِظِينَ ۝ كِرَامًا كَٰتِبِينَ ۝ يَعْلَمُونَ مَا تَفْعَلُونَ ۝

سورة الانفطار: ١٠-١٢

Or do they think that We do not hear their secrets and their private counsels? Rest assured (that We do), and Our messengers are by them to record. (43:80)

أَمْ يَحْسَبُونَ أَنَّا لَا نَسْمَعُ سِرَّهُمْ وَنَجْوَىٰهُم بَلَىٰ وَرُسُلُنَا لَدَيْهِمْ يَكْتُبُونَ ۝

سورة الزخرف: ٨٠

In an amazing two-word sentence, God mentions the two receivers (*al mutalaqqiyān*) who will receive (*yatalaqqā*). He describes them as angels sitting on the right and the left. In the light of modern science, we can appreciate how easily God could record human thoughts and deeds. If receivers are present on either side of the brain's cerebral hemispheres, they can record thoughts and what has been said or done. This could happen in the subconscious. God could program one part of the brain to act as a memory bank of one's actions and thoughts without his awareness. It is just as easy to ask these parts of the brain for an "electronic printout" of their collected data. The brain is a complex electronic network of which vast areas remain unknown. One should not be surprised if, in the afterlife, he is confronted with a book that is a printout of his brain's data banks.

Two (guardian angels), one sitting on the right and the other on the left, are appointed to view and note down (what one does). He cannot utter a word without the sentinel by him (standing) ready (to record it). (50:17-18)

إِذْ يَتَلَقَّى ٱلْمُتَلَقِّيَانِ عَنِ ٱلْيَمِينِ وَعَنِ ٱلشِّمَالِ قَعِيدٌ ۝ مَّا يَلْفِظُ مِن قَوْلٍ إِلَّا لَدَيْهِ رَقِيبٌ عَتِيدٌ ۝

سورة ق: ١٧-١٨

Our record speaks the truth about you, for we recorded everything that you did. (45:29)

هَٰذَا كِتَٰبُنَا يَنطِقُ عَلَيْكُم بِٱلْحَقِّ إِنَّا كُنَّا نَسْتَنسِخُ مَا كُنتُمْ تَعْمَلُونَ ﴿٢٩﴾

سورة الجاثية: ٢٩

What is even more amazing is the fair way in which God records our deeds. Good deeds will outweigh their real value. They could be scored 10 times their value and even, sometimes, 700 times their value. On the other hand, wrong thoughts will not be counted. If one thinks of something bad and does not act, it will not be counted, for only those thoughts actually translated into action will be counted. Our merciful God made the balance in the favor of man. As mentioned earlier, the printout produced for us in the life to come will show all of our life in detail. Who is a better recorder of one's life than his brain?

He who does good shall have it multiplied to his credit ten times. He who does evil shall only be recompensed according to his evil. No wrong shall be done to (either of) them. (6:160)

مَن جَآءَ بِٱلْحَسَنَةِ فَلَهُۥ عَشْرُ أَمْثَالِهَا وَمَن جَآءَ بِٱلسَّيِّئَةِ فَلَا يُجْزَىٰٓ إِلَّا مِثْلَهَا وَهُمْ لَا يُظْلَمُونَ ﴿١٦٠﴾

سورة الأنعام: ١٦٠

Those who spend of their wealth in the way of God are like an ear of corn: it grows seven ears, and each one has one hundred grains. God increases (His blessings) according to His will, cares for all, and knows all things. (2:261)

مَّثَلُ ٱلَّذِينَ يُنفِقُونَ أَمْوَٰلَهُمْ فِى سَبِيلِ ٱللَّهِ كَمَثَلِ حَبَّةٍ أَنۢبَتَتْ سَبْعَ سَنَابِلَ فِى كُلِّ سُنۢبُلَةٍ مِّاْئَةُ حَبَّةٍ وَٱللَّهُ يُضَٰعِفُ لِمَن يَشَآءُ وَٱللَّهُ وَٰسِعٌ عَلِيمٌ ﴿٢٦١﴾

سورة البقرة: ٢٦١

Fingerprints

One of the most difficult tasks for human beings is to find patterns with which to decorate walls, paintings, and so on without falling into the trap of repetition and monotony. However, God has successfully fashioned the tips of human fingers (*banan*) and furnished them with beautiful patterns known as fingerprints. Even more amazing is the fact that no two fingerprints are identical, a fact that has been successfully to identify criminals. One finds it extremely inhibiting, but not surprising, that God will resurrect each person with the same fingerprints.

Does man think that We cannot assemble his bones? We
are able to put together, in perfect order, the very tips of his
fingers! (75:3-4).

أَيَحْسَبُ ٱلْإِنسَـٰنُ أَلَّن نَّجْمَعَ عِظَامَهُ ۝

بَلَىٰ قَـٰدِرِينَ عَلَىٰٓ أَن نُّسَوِّىَ بَنَانَهُ ۝

سورة القيامة: ٣-٤

Human Physiology in Space

This subject has become a progressive field of research over the last
few decades. Most people have experienced a tightness in the chest or a
constriction in the heart when raised in the air by means of either a jet or
a fast elevator. Even more complex physiological studies of the functions
of the heart and respiration had to be investigated before astronauts could
be sent into space. It is amazing how, fourteen centuries ago, tightness in
the chest and constriction in the heart were given as symptoms of elevation into space.

As for those whom God wishes
to guide, He opens their heart
to Islam. As for those whom he
wishes to leave astray, He
makes their heart close and
constricted, as if they were elevated up to the skies. Thus
does God punish those who
refuse to believe. (6:125)

فَمَن يُرِدِ ٱللَّهُ أَن يَهْدِيَهُۥ يَشْرَحْ صَدْرَهُۥ لِلْإِسْلَـٰمِ

وَمَن يُرِدْ أَن يُضِلَّهُۥ يَجْعَلْ صَدْرَهُۥ ضَيِّقًا

حَرَجًا كَأَنَّمَا يَصَّعَّدُ فِى ٱلسَّمَآءِ

كَذَٰلِكَ يَجْعَلُ ٱللَّهُ ٱلرِّجْسَ عَلَى ٱلَّذِينَ

لَا يُؤْمِنُونَ ۝

سورة الأنعام: ١٢٥

It would have been very surprising if God had presented information to
human beings who could not understand what He meant. There was at least
one individual, the prophet Muhammad, who experienced the feeling
described in the verse. Evidence from the Qur'an is almost conclusive. The
surah describing the physiological changes in human respiration and heart
pulsation during elevation was revealed after the surah recording God's
transport of Muhammad from Makkah to Jerusalem and back to Makkah
during the same night (in order of revelation, they were 89th and 67th,
respectively). The physiological description of how one feels upon being
elevated into space is a scientific proof of the night journey. Climbing
mountains, which is slow and laborious, gives a completely different feeling from that of being elevated into space.

Glory to (God), Who took
Muhammad for a night journey
from the Sacred Mosque to the

سُبْحَـٰنَ ٱلَّذِىٓ أَسْرَىٰ بِعَبْدِهِۦ لَيْلًا مِّنَ ٱلْمَسْجِدِ

ٱلْحَرَامِ إِلَى ٱلْمَسْجِدِ ٱلْأَقْصَا ٱلَّذِى بَـٰرَكْنَا حَوْلَهُۥ

Farthest Mosque, whose precincts We have blessed, in order
to show him some of Our signs.
He is the One who hears and
sees (all things). (17:1)

لِنُرِيَهُۥ مِنْ ءَايَـٰتِنَآ إِنَّهُۥ هُوَ ٱلسَّمِيعُ ٱلْبَصِيرُ ١

سورة الإسراء: ١

Post-Natal Care and Infant Mortality

At the time of the Prophet, post-natal care must have been essential to
avoid infant mortality. Sound medical advice would have been crucial for
human survival and preservation. Thus, it is not surprising that God advised
breastfeeding for two years, as this gives the child the antibodies present in
the colostrum and excreted in the mother's milk during the first few days
after delivery. Thereafter, it would provide the baby with a sterile and complete formula of nourishment that would protect it from gastroenteritis,
enteric fever, and other orally transmitted infections. The parents may
decide to wean the baby before the two years pass or to seek a wet nurse.

Mothers shall breastfeed their
young for two years. If (in the
case of divorce) the father wants
this period to be completed, he
shall pay the cost of their food
and clothing on equitable terms.
No person shall have to bear a
burden that is too much for him/
her. No mother shall be treated
unfairly on account of her child,
or a father on account of his
child. An heir shall have the
same responsibilities. If they
both agree on weaning after due
consultation, there is no blame
on them. If you decide on a wet-
nurse for your offspring, there is
no blame on you provided you
pay (her) what you offered on
equitable terms. Be aware of
God and know that He sees
what you do. (2:233)

وَٱلْوَٰلِدَٰتُ يُرْضِعْنَ أَوْلَٰدَهُنَّ حَوْلَيْنِ كَامِلَيْنِ
لِمَنْ أَرَادَ أَن يُتِمَّ ٱلرَّضَاعَةَ وَعَلَى ٱلْمَوْلُودِ لَهُۥ رِزْقُهُنَّ
وَكِسْوَتُهُنَّ بِٱلْمَعْرُوفِ لَا تُكَلَّفُ نَفْسٌ إِلَّا وُسْعَهَا
لَا تُضَآرَّ وَٰلِدَةٌۢ بِوَلَدِهَا وَلَا مَوْلُودٌ لَّهُۥ بِوَلَدِهِۦ
وَعَلَى ٱلْوَارِثِ مِثْلُ ذَٰلِكَ فَإِنْ أَرَادَا فِصَالًا عَن
تَرَاضٍ مِّنْهُمَا وَتَشَاوُرٍ فَلَا جُنَاحَ عَلَيْهِمَا وَإِنْ أَرَدتُّمْ
أَن تَسْتَرْضِعُوٓا۟ أَوْلَٰدَكُمْ فَلَا جُنَاحَ عَلَيْكُمْ إِذَا
سَلَّمْتُم مَّآ ءَاتَيْتُم بِٱلْمَعْرُوفِ وَٱتَّقُوا۟ ٱللَّهَ وَٱعْلَمُوٓا۟
أَنَّ ٱللَّهَ بِمَا تَعْمَلُونَ بَصِيرٌ ٢٣٣

سورة البقرة: ٢٣٣

Human Psychology

Man was not created free of weakness. He is "hasty" and "fretful"
when touched by evil and "gives grudgingly" when good befalls him.

He is created "weak" and "in trouble" and is the most argumentative of creatures.

Man is a creature of haste. I will show him My signs soon (enough). Then you will not ask Me to hasten them. (21:37)

خُلِقَ ٱلْإِنسَـٰنُ مِنْ عَجَلٍ سَأُوْرِيكُمْ ءَايَـٰتِى فَلَا تَسْتَعْجِلُونِ ۝
سورة الأنبياء : ٣٧

Man was created very impatient, frets when evil touches him, and becomes miserly when good reaches him. (70:19-21)

إِنَّ ٱلْإِنسَـٰنَ خُلِقَ هَلُوعًا ۝ إِذَا مَسَّهُ ٱلشَّرُّ جَزُوعًا ۝ وَإِذَا مَسَّهُ ٱلْخَيْرُ مَنُوعًا ۝
سورة المعارج : ١٩–٢١

God wishes to lighten your (difficulties), for man was created weak (in flesh). (4:28)

يُرِيدُ ٱللَّهُ أَن يُخَفِّفَ عَنكُمْ وَخُلِقَ ٱلْإِنسَـٰنُ ضَعِيفًا ۝
سورة النساء : ٢٨

Truly We have created man for toil and struggle. (90:4)

لَقَدْ خَلَقْنَا ٱلْإِنسَـٰنَ فِى كَبَدٍ ۝
سورة البلد : ٤

In this Qur'an We have explained, in detail and for the benefit of mankind, every kind of similitude, yet man is, in most things, contentious. (18:54)

وَلَقَدْ صَرَّفْنَا فِى هَـٰذَا ٱلْقُرْءَانِ لِلنَّاسِ مِن كُلِّ مَثَلٍ وَكَانَ ٱلْإِنسَـٰنُ أَكْثَرَ شَىْءٍ جَدَلًا ۝
سورة الكهف : ٥٤

Our weakness is not limited to these characteristics. We have innate attractions to women (a man craves many sons), gold, silver, pedigree horses, cattle, and crops, namely, all items that our particular society values as sources of wealth. As mentioned earlier, psychologists recognize the presence of our "true unconscious" (the id), which represents the totality of our self-preservative tendencies and instincts. It is this reservoir of instinctive impulses, dominated by the pleasure principle, which could be related to sex, possession, or something else. The Devil seems to play an important role in influencing such instinctive impulses. Remembering God could abort evil thoughts and stop man from being led astray. It seems that the Devil has direct access to our thoughts and can whisper (yuwaswisu) continuously in our ears. We are advised to say God's name before embarking on any important family or business endeavor, for God knows what is in our heart and is nearer to us than our jugular vein.

The things that men love—women, sons, large amounts of gold and silver, pedigree horses, cattle, and fertile land—appear as fair in their eyes. Such are the possessions of this world, but the best of all goals is in nearness to God. (3:14)

زُيِّنَ لِلنَّاسِ حُبُّ ٱلشَّهَوَٰتِ مِنَ ٱلنِّسَآءِ وَٱلْبَنِينَ وَٱلْقَنَٰطِيرِ ٱلْمُقَنطَرَةِ مِنَ ٱلذَّهَبِ وَٱلْفِضَّةِ وَٱلْخَيْلِ ٱلْمُسَوَّمَةِ وَٱلْأَنْعَٰمِ وَٱلْحَرْثِ ۗ ذَٰلِكَ مَتَٰعُ ٱلْحَيَوٰةِ ٱلدُّنْيَا ۖ وَٱللَّهُ عِندَهُۥ حُسْنُ ٱلْمَـَٔابِ ۝
سورة آل عمران: ١٤

From the evil of the one who whispers and then withdraws, the (same) one who whispers into the hearts of men and of jinn. (114:4-6)

مِن شَرِّ ٱلْوَسْوَاسِ ٱلْخَنَّاسِ ۝ ٱلَّذِى يُوَسْوِسُ فِى صُدُورِ ٱلنَّاسِ ۝ مِنَ ٱلْجِنَّةِ وَٱلنَّاسِ ۝
سورة الناس: ٤-٦

Lead (O Satan) to destruction with your (seductive) voice those whom you can. Assault them with your cavalry and infantry. Share with them their wealth and children and make promises to them. But, Satan promises them nothing but deceit. (17:64)

وَٱسْتَفْزِزْ مَنِ ٱسْتَطَعْتَ مِنْهُم بِصَوْتِكَ وَأَجْلِبْ عَلَيْهِم بِخَيْلِكَ وَرَجِلِكَ وَشَارِكْهُمْ فِى ٱلْأَمْوَٰلِ وَٱلْأَوْلَٰدِ وَعِدْهُمْ ۚ وَمَا يَعِدُهُمُ ٱلشَّيْطَٰنُ إِلَّا غُرُورًا ۝
سورة الإسراء: ٦٤

It was We who created man, so We know what dark suggestions his soul makes to him, for we are closer to him than (his) jugular vein. (50:16)

وَلَقَدْ خَلَقْنَا ٱلْإِنسَٰنَ وَنَعْلَمُ مَا تُوَسْوِسُ بِهِۦ نَفْسُهُۥ ۖ وَنَحْنُ أَقْرَبُ إِلَيْهِ مِنْ حَبْلِ ٱلْوَرِيدِ ۝
سورة ق: ١٦

Man is not all evil. The spirit from God that has come down to him via Adam makes him worthy of God's creation. By nature, man likes to be seen as virtuous, a doer of good deeds, kind, helpful, and so on. He always tries his best, even when it is beyond his power. The best example of this is when God offered His trust (amānah) to the heavens, the planet Earth, and the mountains, all of which refused it. Yet man dared to bear this responsibility. This is not an example of man's diligence so much as of his arrogance.

We offered the trust to the heavens, the earth, and the mountains, but they refused to bear it, for they were afraid. Man, however, undertook to bear it—he was indeed unjust and foolish. (33:72)

إِنَّا عَرَضْنَا ٱلْأَمَانَةَ عَلَى ٱلسَّمَٰوَٰتِ وَٱلْأَرْضِ وَٱلْجِبَالِ فَأَبَيْنَ أَن يَحْمِلْنَهَا وَأَشْفَقْنَ مِنْهَا وَحَمَلَهَا ٱلْإِنسَٰنُ ۖ إِنَّهُۥ كَانَ ظَلُومًا جَهُولًا ۝
سورة الأحزاب: ٧٢

Some people are so virtuous and good that God gives them tasks that are far beyond the power of average people. Hence, they require more energy (*rūḥ*) than what has come down to them from Adam. The Qur'an informs us that angels carry this additional energy to them by God's command. Those people have a light that shines around them and makes others accept them as leaders.

You will not find any who believe in God and the Last Day loving those who resist God and His Messenger, even though they were their fathers, sons, brothers, or relatives. For such people, He has implanted faith in their hearts and strengthened them with a spirit from Himself. He will admit them to gardens beneath which rivers flow and in which they will dwell forever. God will be pleased with them, and they will be pleased with Him. They are the party of God. Truly, it is the party of God that will attain success. (58:22)

لَا تَجِدُ قَوْمًا يُؤْمِنُونَ بِٱللَّهِ وَٱلْيَوْمِ ٱلْآخِرِ يُوَآدُّونَ مَنْ حَآدَّ ٱللَّهَ وَرَسُولَهُ وَلَوْ كَانُوٓا ءَابَآءَهُمْ أَوْ أَبْنَآءَهُمْ أَوْ إِخْوَٰنَهُمْ أَوْ عَشِيرَتَهُمْ أُوْلَٰٓئِكَ كَتَبَ فِي قُلُوبِهِمُ ٱلْإِيمَٰنَ وَأَيَّدَهُم بِرُوحٍ مِّنْهُ وَيُدْخِلُهُمْ جَنَّٰتٍ تَجْرِي مِن تَحْتِهَا ٱلْأَنْهَٰرُ خَٰلِدِينَ فِيهَا رَضِيَ ٱللَّهُ عَنْهُمْ وَرَضُوا عَنْهُ أُوْلَٰٓئِكَ حِزْبُ ٱللَّهِ أَلَآ إِنَّ حِزْبَ ٱللَّهِ هُمُ ٱلْمُفْلِحُونَ ﴿٢٢﴾

سورة المجادلة: ٢٢

Raised high above all degrees, He is the Lord of the throne (of authority). By His command does He send the spirit (of inspiration) to any of His servants, in accordance with His will, that it may warn (men) of the Day of Mutual Meeting. (40:15)

رَفِيعُ ٱلدَّرَجَٰتِ ذُو ٱلْعَرْشِ يُلْقِي ٱلرُّوحَ مِنْ أَمْرِهِ عَلَىٰ مَن يَشَآءُ مِنْ عِبَادِهِ لِيُنذِرَ يَوْمَ ٱلتَّلَاقِ ﴿١٥﴾

سورة غافر: ١٥

We have seen that man's body is the site of a continuous reaction between his true unconscious (id) and his virtuous side (the ego and the superego). According to Sigmund Freud, the human mind is divided psychologically into id, ego, and superego. The id is the instinctual element of the human mind and is concerned with pleasure, which demands immediate satisfaction. In addition, it is regarded as the unconscious element of the human psyche and is said to be in conflict with the ego and superego. The ego is a general term for those processes concerned with the self and a person's self-conception and encompasses one's values and attitudes. In Freudian psychology, the term refers specifically to the element of the human mind that represents the conscious processes concerned with reality. It is also in conflict with the id (the instinctual element) and the super-ego (the ethically aware element). The superego is concerned with the ideal and is responsible for ethics and self-imposed standards of behavior. It is characterized as a form of conscience that restrains the ego and is responsible for feelings of guilt when the moral code is broken. God created man with an animal-like body and with all its demands and instincts but gave him a spirit in order to identify him as a human being. God was aware of how great this struggle would be, and this is why He asked the angels to kneel, as a mark of respect, to man.

We told the angels, "Bow down to Adam." All bowed except Iblis, who asked, "Shall I bow down to one whom You created from clay?" (17:61)

وَإِذْ قُلْنَا لِلْمَلَٰٓئِكَةِ ٱسْجُدُوا۟ لِءَادَمَ فَسَجَدُوٓا۟
إِلَّآ إِبْلِيسَ قَالَ ءَأَسْجُدُ لِمَنْ خَلَقْتَ طِينًا ﴿٦١﴾

سورة الإسراء: ٦١

Dreams

There is substantial evidence that God controls one's soul (spirit) during sleep: "He takes human souls during sleep. He holds the souls of those who are doomed to die, and He returns the rest until a specified day."

God takes the souls (of men) when they die and, for those who do not die, He takes their souls while they sleep. Those whose time it is to die are prevented (from returning), but the rest are sent (back to their bodies) for a specific time. In this are signs for those who reflect. (39:42)

ٱللَّهُ يَتَوَفَّى ٱلْأَنفُسَ حِينَ مَوْتِهَا وَٱلَّتِى لَمْ تَمُتْ
فِى مَنَامِهَا فَيُمْسِكُ ٱلَّتِى قَضَىٰ عَلَيْهَا ٱلْمَوْتَ
وَيُرْسِلُ ٱلْأُخْرَىٰٓ إِلَىٰٓ أَجَلٍ مُّسَمًّى إِنَّ فِى ذَٰلِكَ
لَءَايَٰتٍ لِّقَوْمٍ يَتَفَكَّرُونَ ﴿٤٢﴾

سورة الزمر: ٤٢

This verse throws some light on what happens to souls when individuals are asleep. They are not man's possessions, for they are taken by the Creator for reasons unknown. During their journey they wander in the future and the past. There are many dreams recorded in the Qur'an that show souls wandering in the future. However, the soul perceives future events in code, a code that can be revealed only by those who have the right perception and insight.

Remember that in your dream God showed them to you as few. If He had shown them to you as many, you would have been discouraged and would have disputed (your) decision. But God saved (you), for He knows the (secrets) of (all) hearts. (8:43)

إِذْ يُرِيكَهُمُ ٱللَّهُ فِى مَنَامِكَ قَلِيلًا وَلَوْ أَرَىٰكَهُمْ كَثِيرًا لَّفَشِلْتُمْ وَلَتَنَٰزَعْتُمْ فِى ٱلْأَمْرِ وَلَٰكِنَّ ٱللَّهَ سَلَّمَ إِنَّهُۥ عَلِيمٌ بِذَاتِ ٱلصُّدُورِ ﴿٤٣﴾

سورة الأنفال: ٤٣

Two young men entered the prison with him. One of them said, "I dreamed I was pressing wine." The other one said, "I dreamed I was carrying bread on my head and that birds were eating thereof." "Tell us (Yusuf) what our dreams mean, for we see that you are a good man." ... "O my cell-mates, one of you will pour wine for his lord to drink and the other will hang from the cross and birds will eat from his head. [But whatever be your future,] the matter on which you have asked me to enlighten you has been decided [by God]. (12:36, 41)

وَدَخَلَ مَعَهُ ٱلسِّجْنَ فَتَيَانِ قَالَ أَحَدُهُمَآ إِنِّىٓ أَرَىٰنِىٓ أَعْصِرُ خَمْرًا وَقَالَ ٱلْءَاخَرُ إِنِّىٓ أَرَىٰنِىٓ أَحْمِلُ فَوْقَ رَأْسِى خُبْزًا تَأْكُلُ ٱلطَّيْرُ مِنْهُ نَبِّئْنَا بِتَأْوِيلِهِۦٓ إِنَّا نَرَىٰكَ مِنَ ٱلْمُحْسِنِينَ ﴿٣٦﴾

يَٰصَٰحِبَىِ ٱلسِّجْنِ أَمَّآ أَحَدُكُمَا فَيَسْقِى رَبَّهُۥ خَمْرًا وَأَمَّا ٱلْءَاخَرُ فَيُصْلَبُ فَتَأْكُلُ ٱلطَّيْرُ مِن رَّأْسِهِۦ قُضِىَ ٱلْأَمْرُ ٱلَّذِى فِيهِ تَسْتَفْتِيَانِ ﴿٤١﴾

سورة يوسف: ٣٦، ٤١

Diagnosing Pregnancy

Diagnosing pregnancy is now very simple, for the human chorionic gonadotrophin hormone can be detected in plasma or urine. The test can be done in a lab when a period is missed or via a home-testing kit. The fetal heart's beating is visible from the sixth week of pregnancy to real-time ultrasound, can be heard by an ultrasonic detector from the tenth week, and can be heard with an ordinary stethoscope from about the twentieth week. Psuedocyesis (false pregnancy) is usually due to emotional disturbances: intense desire for pregnancy, fear of losing a husband, or desire to achieve parity with other women. This stimulates the hypothalamus and the release of gonadotrophic hormones. A woman complains of regular symptoms, but often in a bizarre order. She will have amenorrhoea (no periods), heavy breasts with a secretion of cloudy fluid from the nipples, and an abdomen enlarged by fat or gas in the stomach or intestines. She will resemble exactly a pregnant woman, but her uterus will not become enlarged. Ultrasound will prove that she is not pregnant.

Many centuries ago, diagnosing pregnancy must have been very difficult and crucial. A man did not know how long to wait before marrying a divorcee or a widow. Marrying a pregnant woman would raise problems of parity and inheritance. God advised two levels of diagnosis here. After her divorce or if she had reached menopause, a woman must wait three months (12 weeks) and not conceal her pregnancy (if any). In the second case, a widow had to wait four months and ten days before marrying again.

Divorcees shall wait three monthly periods (before remarrying) and shall not hide what God has created in their wombs, if they have faith in Him and the Last Day. Their husbands can remarry them during this time if they desire a reconciliation, and the rights of wives [on their husbands] are equal to the [husbands] rights on them, although men have precedence over them [in this respect]. God is Exalted in Power, Wise. (2:228)

وَٱلْمُطَلَّقَٰتُ يَتَرَبَّصْنَ بِأَنفُسِهِنَّ ثَلَٰثَةَ قُرُوٓءٍ وَلَا يَحِلُّ لَهُنَّ أَن يَكْتُمْنَ مَا خَلَقَ ٱللَّهُ فِىٓ أَرْحَامِهِنَّ إِن كُنَّ يُؤْمِنَّ بِٱللَّهِ وَٱلْيَوْمِ ٱلْءَاخِرِ وَبُعُولَتُهُنَّ أَحَقُّ بِرَدِّهِنَّ فِى ذَٰلِكَ إِنْ أَرَادُوٓا۟ إِصْلَٰحًا وَلَهُنَّ مِثْلُ ٱلَّذِى عَلَيْهِنَّ بِٱلْمَعْرُوفِ وَلِلرِّجَالِ عَلَيْهِنَّ دَرَجَةٌ وَٱللَّهُ عَزِيزٌ حَكِيمٌ ۝

سورة البقرة: ٢٢٨

If you have any doubts about those women who no longer menstruate and about those who have no courses, wait for three months. For those who are pregnant, the period begins immediately after they have given birth. For those who are aware of God, He will make their path easy. (65:4)

وَٱلّٰٓـِٔى يَئِسْنَ مِنَ ٱلْمَحِيضِ مِن نِّسَآئِكُمْ إِنِ ٱرْتَبْتُمْ فَعِدَّتُهُنَّ ثَلَٰثَةُ أَشْهُرٍ وَٱلّٰٓـِٔى لَمْ يَحِضْنَ وَأُو۟لَٰتُ ٱلْأَحْمَالِ أَجَلُهُنَّ أَن يَضَعْنَ حَمْلَهُنَّ وَمَن يَتَّقِ ٱللَّهَ يَجْعَل لَّهُۥ مِنْ أَمْرِهِۦ يُسْرًا ۝

سورة الطلاق: ٤

If you die and leave behind widows, they will wait for four months and ten days (before remarrying). When they have completed this time, there is no blame on them if they remarry. God is well acquainted with all that you do. (2:234)

وَٱلَّذِينَ يُتَوَفَّوْنَ مِنكُمْ وَيَذَرُونَ أَزْوَٰجًا يَتَرَبَّصْنَ بِأَنفُسِهِنَّ أَرْبَعَةَ أَشْهُرٍ وَعَشْرًا فَإِذَا بَلَغْنَ أَجَلَهُنَّ فَلَا جُنَاحَ عَلَيْكُمْ فِيمَا فَعَلْنَ فِىٓ أَنفُسِهِنَّ بِٱلْمَعْرُوفِ وَٱللَّهُ بِمَا تَعْمَلُونَ خَبِيرٌ ۝

سورة البقرة: ٢٣٤

The precise time periods given indicate how important it was to determine whether a divorcee or a widow was pregnant. After twelve weeks, there will be a loss of periods, morning sickness, bladder irritability, and changes in the breasts. All of these, as mentioned earlier, can happen in the case of false pregnancy. The only sure sign is the size of the uterus. After twelve weeks, as shown in figure 34, the uterus can be felt in the abdomen above the symphysis pubis. In the case of divorce, the husband would be there and could verify whether or not there had been sexual intercourse prior to the couple's separation and divorce. He would also be able to defend his rights related to his wife's pregnancy and the birth of a live infant. On the other hand, a dead husband could not defend his right of parity to any prospective birth or to testify on sexual relations prior to death. For this reason, God prolonged the period to almost seventeen or eighteen weeks, during which the woman must prove that she is not carrying her deceased husband's child. At this point in her pregnancy, the level of the uterus (fig. 34) will be two fingers breadth below the umbilicus. At about 16 to 18 weeks of pregnancy, a woman who has been pregnant more than once will feel a faint fluttering movement of fetal activity (quickening) (Derek Llewellyn-Jones 1990).

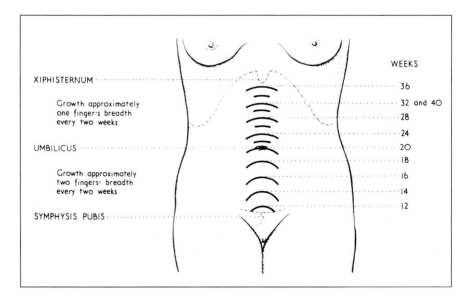

Figure 34: *The abdominal markings of uterine growth related to the number of weeks after the last menstrual period.*

Healthy Sexual Intercourse

Sexual intercourse with women should not take place during menstruation. When her period has passed, the couple can resume its normal sex life.

They ask you about [women's] monthly courses. Say, "It is a vulnerable condition, so keep away from them during their periods and do not approach them until they have cleansed themselves. After they have purified themselves, you may lie with them in any manner, time, or place ordained for you by God. God loves those who turn to Him constantly and those who keep themselves pure and clean." (2:222)

سورة البقرة: ٢٢٢

Intercourse during menses, according to God, may hurt one or both partners. The woman's cervical canal will be open so that her menstrual blood can pass through. It is now known that this condition makes it possible for micro-organisms, especially those that are mobile, to travel up the cervical canal and invade the raw separating endometrium. This may lead to bacteraemia or even septecaemia. The anterior urethra and the prepuce of non-circumcised males are full of bacteria, and sometimes viruses, that may gain access to a woman's circulation and internal organs during intercourse. The man could also be infected by menstrual blood flows carrying vaginal bacteria into his urethra. This could lead to urethritis, prostatitis, epididymitis, and epididymo-orchitis (inflammation of the prostate, epididymis, and testes). Such infections, in the absence of antibiotic treatment, must have been disastrous or even fatal.

God instructs men to lie with women as He has ordained, meaning to avoid routes other than the vagina for intercourse. The vagina is structured for healthy intercourse and causes no harm to either party. The mechanism is very complex yet also extremely effective. For example, there are bacteria in the vagina that keep an acidic environment and act as a disinfectant (similar bacteria can be found in yogurt). A woman's hormonal balance keeps the vagina slightly moist and lubricated. Engaging in sexual activity through other orifices, such as the anus, may prove disastrous.

Physical trauma may occur to either party in the form of tears, ulcers, and even a prolapsed rectum.

Obviously infection, which could be either bacterial or viral, as in herpes genetalis or warts, is a major complication in such relationships. More serious infections could take place in the man's genitalia with a serious outcome. Due to trauma, such blood-born pathogens as Hepatitis B virus infection, Hepatitis C, and Acquired Immune Deficiency Virus (AIDS), among others, could be passed from one partner to the other.

Last but not least, God established the relationship between a man and a woman on love, mercy, and comfort, all of which are essential for human relationships, for these unite the partners for life, ensure continuity, and strengthen the family bond so that children grow up in a happy and healthy environment.

Among His signs is this: He created for you spouses from among yourselves that you may dwell in peace with them, and He has put love and mercy between your (hearts). In this are signs for those who reflect. (30:21)

وَمِنْ ءَايَٰتِهِۦٓ أَنْ خَلَقَ لَكُم مِّنْ أَنفُسِكُمْ أَزْوَٰجًا لِّتَسْكُنُوٓا۟ إِلَيْهَا وَجَعَلَ بَيْنَكُم مَّوَدَّةً وَرَحْمَةً إِنَّ فِى ذَٰلِكَ لَءَايَٰتٍ لِّقَوْمٍ يَتَفَكَّرُونَ ۝

سورة الروم: ٢١

CHAPTER SEVEN

SCIENCES OF MAN

Mathematics, Calendars, and Celestial Navigation

Mathematical sciences have been used by man since the early days of civilization. The design and calculations that allowed the ancient Egyptians to construct the pyramids were advanced and complex even by our modern standards. The ancient Egyptians used three calendars. The first one, based on the moon, was governed by the star Cirius and corresponded to the true solar year. However, it was twelve minutes shorter. Their second calendar, a civil one, was similar to ours and is one quarter of a day shorter than the solar year. Hence, every four years it falls behind the solar year by one day. After the passage of 1,460 years, it will agree with the lunar-solar calendar. The third calendar, which also served as a second lunar calendar although it was based on the civil year and not on the sighting of Cirius, was schematic and artificial. Their calculations were so accurate that the rays of the sun entered the Temple of Abu Simbel and shone in the inner sanctuary on only two days each year: the twenty third of February and twenty third of October. The first celebrates the birthday of Ramses II, and the second is the anniversary of his victory at Kadesh.

The Gregorian calendar is based on the three natural clocks in the sky: the day, the lunar month, and the solar year. It is not very different from the ancient Egyptian civil calendar and is shorter than the solar year by a quarter of a day every year. One day must be added every four years to make up the difference. Sympathy must be given to those born on the twenty ninth of February, as they can celebrate their birthday only once every four years.

Proper mathematical information cannot attain a high level of sophistication unless it is related to time. God informs us that the months that are with Him have been twelve ever since the day He created the heavens and the earth and that the alternation of day and night will help teach mathematics. He created the moon to give light and "determined it into stations" to mark the lunar month. Twelve lunar months formulate a year with God. This is a very strong indication that our calculations should be based on these heavenly clocks.

The number of months (in a year) in the sight of God is twelve. This was ordained by Him the day He created the heavens and the earth. Four of them are sacred. This is the correct usage, so do not wrong yourselves during them. Fight the pagans as a group as they fight you as a group, and know that God is with those who restrain themselves. (9:36)

إِنَّ عِدَّةَ ٱلشُّهُورِ عِندَ ٱللَّهِ ٱثْنَا عَشَرَ شَهْرًا فِى كِتَٰبِ ٱللَّهِ يَوْمَ خَلَقَ ٱلسَّمَٰوَٰتِ وَٱلْأَرْضَ مِنْهَآ أَرْبَعَةٌ حُرُمٌ ذَٰلِكَ ٱلدِّينُ ٱلْقَيِّمُ فَلَا تَظْلِمُوا۟ فِيهِنَّ أَنفُسَكُمْ وَقَٰتِلُوا۟ ٱلْمُشْرِكِينَ كَآفَّةً كَمَا يُقَٰتِلُونَكُمْ كَآفَّةً وَٱعْلَمُوٓا۟ أَنَّ ٱللَّهَ مَعَ ٱلْمُتَّقِينَ ﴿٣٦﴾

سورة التوبة: ٣٦

It is He who made the sun a shining glory and the moon a light (of beauty). He measured out stages for it so that you might know the number of years and the count (of time). God created all of this in truth and righteousness. He explains His signs in detail for those who understand. (10:5)

هُوَ ٱلَّذِى جَعَلَ ٱلشَّمْسَ ضِيَآءً وَٱلْقَمَرَ نُورًا وَقَدَّرَهُۥ مَنَازِلَ لِتَعْلَمُوا۟ عَدَدَ ٱلسِّنِينَ وَٱلْحِسَابَ مَا خَلَقَ ٱللَّهُ ذَٰلِكَ إِلَّا بِٱلْحَقِّ يُفَصِّلُ ٱلْءَايَٰتِ لِقَوْمٍ يَعْلَمُونَ ﴿٥﴾

سورة يونس: ٥

We have made the night and the day as two (of Our) signs. We have obscured the sign of the night, whereas We have made the sign of the day to enlighten you, so you may seek the bounty of God and so you may know the number and count of the years. We have explained all things in detail. (17:12)

وَجَعَلْنَا ٱلَّيْلَ وَٱلنَّهَارَ ءَايَتَيْنِ فَمَحَوْنَآ ءَايَةَ ٱلَّيْلِ وَجَعَلْنَآ ءَايَةَ ٱلنَّهَارِ مُبْصِرَةً لِّتَبْتَغُوا۟ فَضْلًا مِّن رَّبِّكُمْ وَلِتَعْلَمُوا۟ عَدَدَ ٱلسِّنِينَ وَٱلْحِسَابَ وَكُلَّ شَىْءٍ فَصَّلْنَٰهُ تَفْصِيلًا ﴿١٢﴾

سورة الإسراء: ١٢

Celestial Navigation

Before the invention of the compass, people could only find their way by means of celestial navigation. From the different phases of the moon and its position in the sky, as well as from the different positions of the sun, people could identify direction during the day and the night. Stars, especially those arranged in constellations and that assume varied positions during the year, were used to navigate on land and sea. However, the real problem was to find a celestial body with a constant and recognizable path that could be related to other celestial bodies. The answer to this problem was emphasized in the Qur'an: the stages of the moon make one lunar month and twelve lunar months make one year. Hence, the Arab calendar was and remains based on the lunar month.

Accumulated information based on moon sightings and other celestial bodies is collected in an almanac (derived from Arabic *al manakh* [weather, climate, and changes in natural phenomena]). Almanacs are used to navigate at sea, in the air, and in space. A ship captain can plan his course in advance and plot his course and position at sea on different days by means of an almanac. It also gives him the precise position of the moon and stars at any time in the future. At sea, his boat's position could be readjusted during the journey by taking bearings from existing celestial bodies and adjusting for wind, tide, current, and other weather-related phenomenon.

Traditional navigational methods include the use of a magnetic compass and a sextant. Today, the gyrocompass meets this need, along with highly sophisticated electronic methods employing beacons of radio signals, such as DECCA (accuracy of 50 meters at a range of 180 kms.) and OMEGA (accuracy of 4 kms. during the day and 7 kms. at night). Satellite navigation uses satellites that broadcast time and position signals. The United States Global Positioning System (GPS) has an accuracy of 100 meters and can also be used by pedestrians and motorists. In 1992, 85 nations agreed to take part in trials of a new navigation system. Future Navigation System (FANS) will make use of the 24 Russian Glonass satellites and the 24 American GPS satellites. Small computers will gradually be fitted to civil aircraft, so they can process the satellites' signals. The signals from at least 3 satellites will guide the craft to within a few meters of accuracy. FANS will be used in conjunction with 4 Imarsat satellites to provide worldwide communication between pilots and air-traffic controllers.

This modern degree of sophistication in navigation would never have been reached without the earlier use of celestial bodies. Man has replaced the moon, the sun, and the stars with satellites to guide his way.

Blessed is He Who made constellations in the skies, and placed therein a [radiant] lamp and a light-giving moon. (25:61)

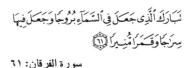

تَبَارَكَ ٱلَّذِى جَعَلَ فِى ٱلسَّمَآءِ بُرُوجًا وَجَعَلَ فِيهَا سِرَٰجًا وَقَمَرًا مُّنِيرًا ٦١

سورة الفرقان: ٦١

God separates the daybreak (from the dark), makes the night for rest and peace, and the sun and moon for the reckoning (of time). Such is His judgment and ordering. (He is) Exalted in Power, the Om-niscient. It is God who makes the stars (as beacons) for you, so that you can guide yourselves with their help through the dark spaces of the land and sea. We detail Our signs for people who know. (6:96-97)

فَالِقُ ٱلْإِصْبَاحِ وَجَعَلَ ٱلَّيْلَ سَكَنًا وَٱلشَّمْسَ وَٱلْقَمَرَ حُسْبَانًا ذَٰلِكَ تَقْدِيرُ ٱلْعَزِيزِ ٱلْعَلِيمِ ۝ وَهُوَ ٱلَّذِى جَعَلَ لَكُمُ ٱلنُّجُومَ لِتَهْتَدُوا۟ بِهَا فِى ظُلُمَٰتِ ٱلْبَرِّ وَٱلْبَحْرِ قَدْ فَصَّلْنَا ٱلْآيَٰتِ لِقَوْمٍ يَعْلَمُونَ ۝

سورة الأنعام: ٩٦-٩٧

Wind Control

The atmosphere is in constant motion. The chief reason for its move-ment is the heat produced by the sun, which, being the most concentrated around the equator, heats the air at the equator. This air then expands and rises, a process that creates a low-pressure area into which tradewinds blow from north and south. This low-pressure area around the equator is often called the doldrums. The warm air from the equator cools as it rises, spreads north and south, and then finally sinks back to the ground around a latitude of 30° north and 30° south. The descending air creates high-pres-sure regions, known as the horse latitudes, in these latitudes. Part of the air from these latitudes flows back to the equator while another part flows toward the poles, where it meets cold dense air. In these ways, winds redistribute heat around the earth.

Air currents do not flow from north to south, for they are deflected by the Coriolis force. This force is caused by Earth's rotation and is similar to the effect achieved if one runs a piece of chalk straight down a spinning globe from north to south. When one stops the globe, one will find that the line is curved. Due to the Coriolis force, winds in the northern hemisphere are deflected to the right of the direction in which they are blowing, while winds in the southern hemisphere are deflected to the left. As a result, winds blowing into the equatorial doldrums from the south become north-east tradewinds, and winds in the southern hemisphere become south-east tradewinds. Winds flowing north from the northern horse latitudes become south-westerlies, and winds blowing south from the southern horse lati-tudes become north-westerlies.

During the summer, winds blow from the sea toward the land. In the winter, this process is reversed. A similar process can be seen, to a lesser degree, during the day and the night. In many areas, local winds play a major role, such as the cold Mistral wind in the Rhône Valley, the warm Chinook wind in Canada, and many others. Winds move the clouds that could bring rain, depending on the temperature, humidity, and latitude.

Does this all just happen by coincidence, or is someone in control? It must be controlled by a supernatural power that ensures their continuity (45:5). In England, it has been established that rain falls every year and that the country would become a desert if it did not (35:9). God is the only power that can decide the fate of nations. He has done so in the past and will continue to do so in the future. History provides us with several examples of nations that have disappeared due to a radical climactic change. The presence of oil in desert countries is strong evidence that such land, at some point in the past, must have been fertile and covered with trees.

In the alternation of the night and the day, and the fact that God sends down sustenance from the sky and revives therewith the dead earth, and in the change of the winds, are signs for those who are wise. (45:5)

وَٱخْتِلَٰفِ ٱلَّيْلِ وَٱلنَّهَارِ وَمَآ أَنزَلَ ٱللَّهُ مِنَ ٱلسَّمَآءِ مِن رِّزْقٍ فَأَحْيَا بِهِ ٱلْأَرْضَ بَعْدَ مَوْتِهَا وَتَصْرِيفِ ٱلرِّيَٰحِ ءَايَٰتٌ لِّقَوْمٍ يَعْقِلُونَ ۝

سورة الجاثية: ٥

It is God who sends the winds to raise the clouds. Then We send them to a land that is dead and revive it therewith. Even so (will be) the resurrection. (35:9)

وَٱللَّهُ ٱلَّذِىٓ أَرْسَلَ ٱلرِّيَٰحَ فَتُثِيرُ سَحَابًا فَسُقْنَٰهُ إِلَىٰ بَلَدٍ مَّيِّتٍ فَأَحْيَيْنَا بِهِ ٱلْأَرْضَ بَعْدَ مَوْتِهَا كَذَٰلِكَ ٱلنُّشُورُ ۝

سورة فاطر: ٩

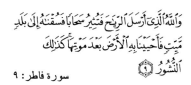

Supersonic Waves

The speed of sound was reached in 1947 by an American Air Force officer and also in 1948 by RAF Squadron Leader John Derry (in a DeHaviland 108 research aircraft). During the Second World War, sonic waves were used to detect submarines and other ships. Subsequently, they were used in metallurgy and then in medicine to diagnose pregnant women who were carrying twins, triplets, or more embryos. Such advanced techniques as sonography are now used to image vessels and an individual's internal organs.

This practice was, by no means, the first in the world, for bats use an echo-locating system to pinpoint their prey and to avoid obstacles while in flight. Contrary to popular belief, bats are not entirely blind: they can see in twilight. In the darkness they send out high-frequency squeaks, only some of which are audible to man. The returning echoes tell the exact position of any obstacle. They fly in groups of thousands but respond to their own individual echo-signals and are not confused by other noises. Scientists have tried to jam these radar signals by aiming at them noise two thousand times more intense than theirs and at the same frequency—it did not disturb them at all. High frequency sound waves have been used to destroy bacteria and other micro-organisms, to prepare bacterial antigens, and to prepare vaccines. Man is still very primitive when it comes to using sound.

God has used sound to destroy nations (15:83: 11:94; 11:67). Moreover, He will use it to destroy the planet on the Day of Doom (39:68) and to raise everyone from the dead (39:68; 36:51, 53). Thus, sound can both destroy and reconstruct human beings. This is a completely new application that may prove very valuable as a new area of research.

But the (mighty) blast seized them during the morning. (15:83)

فَأَخَذَتْهُمُ ٱلصَّيْحَةُ مُصْبِحِينَ ۝

سورة الحجر : ٨٣

After We issued Our decree, We saved Shu'ayb and those who believed with him by a (special) mercy from Ourselves. But the (mighty) blast seized the wrong-doers, and they lay prostrate in their homes by the morning. (11:94)

وَلَمَّا جَآءَ أَمْرُنَا نَجَّيْنَا شُعَيْبًا وَٱلَّذِينَ ءَامَنُوا۟ مَعَهُۥ بِرَحْمَةٍ مِّنَّا وَأَخَذَتِ ٱلَّذِينَ ظَلَمُوا۟ ٱلصَّيْحَةُ فَأَصْبَحُوا۟ فِى دِيَٰرِهِمْ جَٰثِمِينَ ۝

سورة هود: ٩٤

The (mighty) blast overtook the wrong-doers, and they lay prostrate in their homes before the morning. (11:67)

وَأَخَذَ ٱلَّذِينَ ظَلَمُوا۟ ٱلصَّيْحَةُ فَأَصْبَحُوا۟ فِى دِيَٰرِهِمْ جَٰثِمِينَ ۝

سورة هود: ٦٧

The trumpet will be sounded, and then all that is in the heavens and on the earth will swoon, except those whom God will decide (to exempt). Then a second one will be sounded when they will be standing and looking on. (39:68)

وَنُفِخَ فِى ٱلصُّورِ فَصَعِقَ مَن فِى ٱلسَّمَٰوَٰتِ وَمَن فِى ٱلْأَرْضِ إِلَّا مَن شَآءَ ٱللَّهُ ثُمَّ نُفِخَ فِيهِ أُخْرَىٰ فَإِذَا هُمْ قِيَامٌ يَنظُرُونَ ۝

سورة الزمر : ٦٨

The trumpet shall be sounded, and (men) will rush forth from the sepulchers to their Lord. .... It will be no more than a single blast, after which they will all be brought up before Us. (36:51, 53)

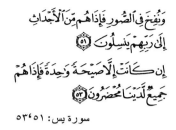

سورة يس: ٥١٬٥٣

The Weight of an Atom

Until very recently, the atom was thought to be the smallest portion of matter in existence and also indivisible. This was the belief in all schools during the 1940s. It was discovered only later that atomic fission was possible.

God has always referred to the smallest particle of matter as "the weight of an atom" (34:22) and uses it to symbolize a very small weight (4:40; 99:7-8). What is even more interesting is the existence of smaller particles weighing even less than an atom, and that God knows where every atom is and keeps such information in a register (34:3;10:61). He has stores of matter from which He releases various portions in known measures as and when required (15:21). Wherever it may be in the heavens, on Earth, in rock, or elsewhere, He can retrieve it (31:16).

Bacteria are labeled by the viruses that live on them, a phenomenon known as "bacteriophage typing." It is also possible to identify viruses by their nucleic acid (DNA), which is called "genotypic sequencing." The power of labeling atoms and their particles is incomprehensible. The verses related above imply that God has labeled all atoms, as well as their particles, of different matter. If they can all be labeled, they must all be different. Modern science may shed some light on this mystery.

It was shown earlier that the proton located inside the nucleus of a hydrogen atom can be identified by Magnetic Resonance Imaging (MRI). Recently, it was proven that the magnetic field located at the nucleus is determined largely by the external magnetic field. The intensity of the magnetic field located at the nucleus is a function of the electrons immediately surrounding the nucleus and is also influenced by the electrons of adjacent atoms. The interaction of the electrons with the external field, which causes the alteration of the field located at the site of the nucleus, gives rise to what is called a "chemical shift." Therefore, at a given external field, every chemically distinct nucleus of a given species resonates at a slightly different frequency. This causes the appearance of different magnetic resonance peaks, which can be viewed by means of Magnetic

Resonance Spectroscopy (MRS). Just as MRI produces an anatomical image, MRS yields quantitative chemical information. This can now be provided in an imaging format and is referred to as Magnetic Resonance Spectroscopic Imaging (MRSI).

So, although the nuclei of different elements are made of protons that are basically similar, the effect on them of the surrounding external electrons, as well as those of adjacent atoms, causes them to produce resonances of different frequencies that can be differentiated. This and many other techniques are available to the Creator, especially if all the particles are in a register. On the Day of Resurrection, God will have no problem in reconstructing every living body.

Say, "Call upon those (gods) other than God, in whom you believe. They have no power, not even the weight of an atom, in the heavens or on the earth. They have no share therein, nor is any of them a helper to God." (34:22)

قُلِ ٱدْعُواْ ٱلَّذِينَ زَعَمْتُم مِّن دُونِ ٱللَّهِ لَا يَمْلِكُونَ مِثْقَالَ ذَرَّةٍ فِي ٱلسَّمَٰوَٰتِ وَلَا فِي ٱلْأَرْضِ وَمَا لَهُمْ فِيهِمَا مِن شِرْكٍ وَمَا لَهُ مِنْهُم مِّن ظَهِيرٍ ۝

سورة سبأ: ٢٢

God does nothing unjust, not even to the weight of an atom. If (one does) a good deed, He multiplies it and gives (the doer of good) a great reward. (4:40)

إِنَّ ٱللَّهَ لَا يَظْلِمُ مِثْقَالَ ذَرَّةٍ وَإِن تَكُ حَسَنَةً يُضَٰعِفْهَا وَيُؤْتِ مِن لَّدُنْهُ أَجْرًا عَظِيمًا ۝

سورة النساء: ٤٠

One who has done (even) an atom's weight of good will see it, and one who has done (even) an atom's weight of evil will see it. (99:7-8)

فَمَن يَعْمَلْ مِثْقَالَ ذَرَّةٍ خَيْرًا يَرَهُۥ ۝ وَمَن يَعْمَلْ مِثْقَالَ ذَرَّةٍ شَرًّا يَرَهُۥ ۝

سورة الزلزلة: ٧-٨

The unbelievers say, "The Hour will never reach us." Say, "Of course it will reach you. By my Lord, by the One who knows the unseen, from whom not even the least atom in the heavens or on the earth is hidden, it will come to you. Regardless of size, everything is recorded in a clear record." (34:3)

وَقَالَ ٱلَّذِينَ كَفَرُواْ لَا تَأْتِينَا ٱلسَّاعَةُ قُلْ بَلَىٰ وَرَبِّي لَتَأْتِيَنَّكُمْ عَٰلِمِ ٱلْغَيْبِ لَا يَعْزُبُ عَنْهُ مِثْقَالُ ذَرَّةٍ فِي ٱلسَّمَٰوَٰتِ وَلَا فِي ٱلْأَرْضِ وَلَا أَصْغَرُ مِن ذَٰلِكَ وَلَا أَكْبَرُ إِلَّا فِي كِتَٰبٍ مُّبِينٍ ۝

سورة سبأ: ٣

In whatever business you may be engaged, in whatever portion of the Qur'an you may be reciting, and whatever you many be doing, (remember) O mankind, that when you are deeply engrossed therein, We see what you are doing. Nothing is hidden from God, not even the weight of an atom on the earth or in heaven, and everything is recorded in a clear record. (10:61)

وَمَا تَكُونُ فِى شَأْنٍ وَمَا تَتْلُوا مِنْهُ مِن قُرْءَانٍ وَلَا تَعْمَلُونَ مِنْ عَمَلٍ إِلَّا كُنَّا عَلَيْكُمْ شُهُودًا إِذْ تُفِيضُونَ فِيهِ وَمَا يَعْزُبُ عَن رَّبِّكَ مِن مِّثْقَالِ ذَرَّةٍ فِى ٱلْأَرْضِ وَلَا فِى ٱلسَّمَآءِ وَلَآ أَصْغَرَ مِن ذَٰلِكَ وَلَآ أَكْبَرَ إِلَّا فِى كِتَٰبٍ مُّبِينٍ ٦١

سورة يونس : ٦١

And there is nothing but its (sources) and (inexhaustible) treasures are with Us, but We only send down (what is necessary) in due and ascertainable measure. (15:21)

وَإِن مِّن شَىْءٍ إِلَّا عِندَنَا خَزَآئِنُهُ وَمَا نُنَزِّلُهُ إِلَّا بِقَدَرٍ مَّعْلُومٍ ٢١

سورة الحجر : ٢١

"My son," (said Luqman), "anything, even if it were to have the weight of a mustard seed and be (hidden) in a rock or (elsewhere) in the heavens or on the earth, will be brought forth by God, for He understands the finer mysteries (and) is well-acquainted (with them)." (31:16)

يَٰبُنَىَّ إِنَّهَآ إِن تَكُ مِثْقَالَ حَبَّةٍ مِّنْ خَرْدَلٍ فَتَكُن فِى صَخْرَةٍ أَوْ فِى ٱلسَّمَٰوَٰتِ أَوْ فِى ٱلْأَرْضِ يَأْتِ بِهَا ٱللَّهُ إِنَّ ٱللَّهَ لَطِيفٌ خَبِيرٌ ١٦

سورة لقمان : ١٦

Statistics

At the beginning, man started with simple statistics, such as the recording of births and deaths. Later on, he moved gradually to the calculator, the sorting machine, and the computer. Unfortunately, the accuracy of the data entered depends on the care with which it is gathered and interpreted by its human collector(s). Regardless of its sophistication, the computer is liable to human error, a condition that affects the accuracy and outcome of the resulting statistics. For example, even the most "accurate" census undertaken by the most advanced country will miss many people and leave many facts unrecorded .

God has emphasized repeatedly the importance of statistics. He keeps records not just on human beings but on everything in His universe.

He takes account of them (all) and has numbered everything exactly. (19:94)

لَقَدۡ أَحۡصَىٰهُمۡ وَعَدَّهُمۡ عَدًّا ۝

سورة مريم: ٩٤

So that He may know that they have brought and delivered the messages of their Lord, He surrounds (all the mysteries) that are with them and takes account of everything. (72:28)

لِّيَعۡلَمَ أَن قَدۡ أَبۡلَغُوا۟ رِسَٰلَٰتِ رَبِّهِمۡ وَأَحَاطَ بِمَا لَدَيۡهِمۡ وَأَحۡصَىٰ كُلَّ شَىۡءٍ عَدَدًۢا ۝

سورة الجن: ٢٨

We shall give life to the dead. We record all that they have done and the consequences of their actions, which remain after their death. We have taken account of everything in a clear record. (36:12)

إِنَّا نَحۡنُ نُحۡىِ ٱلۡمَوۡتَىٰ وَنَكۡتُبُ مَا قَدَّمُوا۟ وَءَاثَٰرَهُمۡ وَكُلَّ شَىۡءٍ أَحۡصَيۡنَٰهُ فِىٓ إِمَامٍ مُّبِينٍ ۝

سورة يس: ١٢

Then are men returned to God, their true Protector. To Him belongs the command, and He is the swiftest when it comes to taking account (of what they have done). (6:62)

ثُمَّ رُدُّوٓا۟ إِلَى ٱللَّهِ مَوۡلَىٰهُمُ ٱلۡحَقِّ أَلَا لَهُ ٱلۡحُكۡمُ وَهُوَ أَسۡرَعُ ٱلۡحَٰسِبِينَ ۝

سورة الأنعام: ٦٢

Pairs

Strong evidence has been given in the Qur'an that God has created everything in pairs. Thus, one should always look for pairs in matter and non-matter. This statement is very useful for scientists. For example, electricity and magnetism are present in pairs of positive and negative. It has also been shown by Hawking that, according to quantum mechanics, space contains "virtual particles" and "anti-particles." Perhaps these represent stores of matter in space.

We have created everything in pairs so that you might receive instruction. (51:49)

وَمِن كُلِّ شَىۡءٍ خَلَقۡنَا زَوۡجَيۡنِ لَعَلَّكُمۡ تَذَكَّرُونَ ۝

سورة الذاريات: ٤٩

Glory to God, Who created in pairs all that the earth produces, as well as human beings and (other) things of which they have no knowledge. (36:36)

سُبۡحَٰنَ ٱلَّذِى خَلَقَ ٱلۡأَزۡوَٰجَ كُلَّهَا مِمَّا تُنۢبِتُ ٱلۡأَرۡضُ وَمِنۡ أَنفُسِهِمۡ وَمِمَّا لَا يَعۡلَمُونَ ۝

سورة يس: ٣٦

Language and Communication

Animals and birds have their own forms of language. For example, scientists have communicated with dolphins, and whales have been shown to be very intelligent and to have a complex communication system known as songs. The killer whale in the wild has 8 to 15 special calls, and each family group (pod) has a particular dialect. They are the first mammals known to have dialects, as is the case with man. Bees transmit data to each other about food sources by a dance, each movement of which gives rise to sound impulses picked up by tiny hairs located on the back of its head. The dance's orientation is also significant. God said that animals and birds, like man, are nations that communicate in their own language (6:38) and that ants have a language that Solomon could understand (27:18-19).

All animals (that live) on the earth and that fly on their wings (form part of) communities like you. We have omitted nothing from the Book, and (all of) them shall be gathered to their Lord in the end. (6:38)

وَمَا مِن دَآبَّةٍ فِى ٱلْأَرْضِ وَلَا طَٰٓئِرٍ يَطِيرُ بِجَنَاحَيْهِ إِلَّآ أُمَمٌ أَمْثَالُكُم مَّا فَرَّطْنَا فِى ٱلْكِتَٰبِ مِن شَىْءٍ ثُمَّ إِلَىٰ رَبِّهِمْ يُحْشَرُونَ ﴿٣٨﴾

سورة الأنعام: ٣٨

The seven heavens and the earth, and all beings therein, declare His glory. Everything celebrates His praise, although you do not understand how they declare His glory. Truly, He is Oft-Forbearing, Most Forgiving. (17:44)

تُسَبِّحُ لَهُ ٱلسَّمَٰوَٰتُ ٱلسَّبْعُ وَٱلْأَرْضُ وَمَن فِيهِنَّ وَإِن مِّن شَىْءٍ إِلَّا يُسَبِّحُ بِحَمْدِهِ وَلَٰكِن لَّا تَفْقَهُونَ تَسْبِيحَهُمْ إِنَّهُ كَانَ حَلِيمًا غَفُورًا ﴿٤٤﴾

سورة الإسراء: ٤٤

When they came to a (low) valley of ants, one of the ants said, "Fellow ants, go into your homes lest Solomon and his soldiers crush you (underfoot) unknowingly." Solomon smiled, amused by the speech, and said, "O my Lord. Inspire me to be grateful for the favors You have bestowed on me and my parents, and (inspire me) to lead a righteous life that will please You. Admit me, by Your grace, to the ranks of Your righteous servants." (27:18-19)

حَتَّىٰٓ إِذَآ أَتَوْا عَلَىٰ وَادِ ٱلنَّمْلِ قَالَتْ نَمْلَةٌ يَٰٓأَيُّهَا ٱلنَّمْلُ ٱدْخُلُوا مَسَٰكِنَكُمْ لَا يَحْطِمَنَّكُمْ سُلَيْمَٰنُ وَجُنُودُهُ وَهُمْ لَا يَشْعُرُونَ ﴿١٨﴾ فَتَبَسَّمَ ضَاحِكًا مِّن قَوْلِهَا وَقَالَ رَبِّ أَوْزِعْنِىٓ أَنْ أَشْكُرَ نِعْمَتَكَ ٱلَّتِىٓ أَنْعَمْتَ عَلَىَّ وَعَلَىٰ وَٰلِدَىَّ وَأَنْ أَعْمَلَ صَٰلِحًا تَرْضَىٰهُ وَأَدْخِلْنِى بِرَحْمَتِكَ فِى عِبَادِكَ ٱلصَّٰلِحِينَ ﴿١٩﴾

سورة النمل: ١٨-١٩

Light

People have always known that light comes from the sun, the moon, the stars, lightning, and fire. Perhaps they did not realize that lightning creates a very strong electric charge that can kill people by means of electric shock (13:13). Electricity has been demonstrated to man through animals. For example, the electric eel, which lives in South American rivers, can produce enough electricity to light more than a dozen electric lightbulbs. It releases from its tail 600 volts, which, at a current of approximately 2 amps, is enough to kill its prey by shock. The electric eel can reach six feet in length and, when it moves, sends out weak electric impulses from two small pilot "batteries" to detect unseen prey or enemies. This creates an electric field around the eel, and any change in it will inform the eel of the intruder's size and position.

Electric fish are found in rivers and oceans in various parts of the world. The fresh water electric cat fish of tropical Africa paralyses or kills its prey with a shock of up to several hundred volts discharged from a membrane located along its back. The disc-shaped electric ray of the Atlantic and Indian oceans and the Mediterranean, a member of the shark family, can stun or kill smaller fish but cannot harm humans. From the firefly, man saw how light could be produced by chemical reactions. Unlike lightbulbs, the light produced has no heat energy and is far more efficient than an electric bulb.

Evidence has been given to man that light can be produced without fire. It already existed when God gave the example of His own light. It is up to man to unveil its secrets.

Thunder repeats His praise, as do the angels, with awe. He flings loud-voiced thunderbolts and, with them, strikes whoever He wills. And yet these (men dare to) dispute with God over the strength of His (supreme) power. (13:13)

وَيُسَبِّحُ ٱلرَّعْدُ بِحَمْدِهِۦ وَٱلْمَلَٰٓئِكَةُ مِنْ خِيفَتِهِۦ وَيُرْسِلُ ٱلصَّوَٰعِقَ فَيُصِيبُ بِهَا مَن يَشَآءُ وَهُمْ يُجَٰدِلُونَ فِى ٱللَّهِ وَهُوَ شَدِيدُ ٱلْمِحَالِ ﴿١٣﴾

سورة الرعد: ١٣

God is the light of the heavens and the earth. The parable of His light is thus: there is a niche, and within it a lamp, the lamp enclosed in glass, the

ٱللَّهُ نُورُ ٱلسَّمَٰوَٰتِ وَٱلْأَرْضِ مَثَلُ نُورِهِۦ كَمِشْكَوٰةٍ فِيهَا مِصْبَاحٌ ٱلْمِصْبَاحُ فِى زُجَاجَةٍ ٱلزُّجَاجَةُ كَأَنَّهَا كَوْكَبٌ دُرِّيٌّ يُوقَدُ مِن شَجَرَةٍ

glass a brilliant star lit from a blessed tree—an olive tree—neither of the East nor the West, whose oil is luminous, though fire hardly touches it. Light upon light. God guides whom He will to His light. He sets forth parables for men, and He knows all things. (24:35)

مُّبَٰرَكَةٖ زَيۡتُونَةٖ لَّا شَرۡقِيَّةٖ وَلَا غَرۡبِيَّةٖ يَكَادُ زَيۡتُهَا

يُضِيٓءُ وَلَوۡ لَمۡ تَمۡسَسۡهُ نَارٞ نُّورٌ عَلَىٰ نُورٖ يَهۡدِى

ٱللَّهُ لِنُورِهِۦ مَن يَشَآءُ وَيَضۡرِبُ ٱللَّهُ ٱلۡأَمۡثَٰلَ

لِلنَّاسِ وَٱللَّهُ بِكُلِّ شَىۡءٍ عَلِيمٞ ﴿٣٥﴾

سورة النور: ٣٥

Hygiene

Water was very scarce in the deserts of Arabia at the time of the Qur'an's revelation. A person living at that time probably would have considered it the most valuable object in the area. However, God has asked people to wash before prayers, and, in its absence, to use "wholesome dust" and behave as if they were washing their hands and face. This was done to implant the habit of cleanliness in man (5:6). Rainwater was described as pure (25:48), an assertion that has now been revealed as true, for it is virtually distilled water with very few impurities from the air through which it passes. He advised people to use it to purify themselves (8:11). If people only consumed rainwater, they would not be infected by water-borne diseases. Britain relies on rainwater for its drinking water and collects it in large reservoirs for this purpose. Unfortunately, it becomes polluted as it flows downhill to the reservoirs.

It is God Who sends the winds as heralds of glad tidings, going before His mercy, and We send down pure water from the sky. (25:48)

وَهُوَ ٱلَّذِىٓ أَرۡسَلَ ٱلرِّيَٰحَ بُشۡرَۢا بَيۡنَ يَدَىۡ

رَحۡمَتِهِۦ وَأَنزَلۡنَا مِنَ ٱلسَّمَآءِ مَآءٗ طَهُورٗا ﴿٤٨﴾

سورة الفرقان: ٤٨

Remember that He covered you with a sort of drowsiness in order to make you calm, and that He caused rain from heaven to fall upon you in order to cleanse you and to remove from you the stain of Satan, to strengthen your hearts, and to plant your feet firmly therewith. (8:11)

إِذۡ يُغَشِّيكُمُ ٱلنُّعَاسَ أَمَنَةٗ مِّنۡهُ وَيُنَزِّلُ عَلَيۡكُم

مِّنَ ٱلسَّمَآءِ مَآءٗ لِّيُطَهِّرَكُم بِهِۦ وَيُذۡهِبَ عَنكُمۡ

رِجۡزَ ٱلشَّيۡطَٰنِ وَلِيَرۡبِطَ عَلَىٰ قُلُوبِكُمۡ

وَيُثَبِّتَ بِهِ ٱلۡأَقۡدَامَ ﴿١١﴾

سورة الأنفال: ١١

O believers, when you prepare for prayer wash your faces and your hands (and arms) up to the elbows. Rub your heads (with water) and (wash) your feet to the ankles. If you are in a state of ritual impurity, wash your whole body. If you are sick, traveling, answering the call of nature, or have had (sexual) relations with women and can find no water, use clean sand or earth and rub your faces and hands with it. God does not want to make things hard on you, but to make you clean and to complete His favor to you so that you may be grateful. (5:6)

يَٰٓأَيُّهَا ٱلَّذِينَ ءَامَنُوٓاْ إِذَا قُمۡتُمۡ إِلَى ٱلصَّلَوٰةِ فَٱغۡسِلُواْ وُجُوهَكُمۡ وَأَيۡدِيَكُمۡ إِلَى ٱلۡمَرَافِقِ وَٱمۡسَحُواْ بِرُءُوسِكُمۡ وَأَرۡجُلَكُمۡ إِلَى ٱلۡكَعۡبَيۡنِۚ وَإِن كُنتُمۡ جُنُبٗا فَٱطَّهَّرُواْۚ وَإِن كُنتُم مَّرۡضَىٰٓ أَوۡ عَلَىٰ سَفَرٍ أَوۡ جَآءَ أَحَدٞ مِّنكُم مِّنَ ٱلۡغَآئِطِ أَوۡ لَٰمَسۡتُمُ ٱلنِّسَآءَ فَلَمۡ تَجِدُواْ مَآءٗ فَتَيَمَّمُواْ صَعِيدٗا طَيِّبٗا فَٱمۡسَحُواْ بِوُجُوهِكُمۡ وَأَيۡدِيكُم مِّنۡهُۚ مَا يُرِيدُ ٱللَّهُ لِيَجۡعَلَ عَلَيۡكُم مِّنۡ حَرَجٖ وَلَٰكِن يُرِيدُ لِيُطَهِّرَكُمۡ وَلِيُتِمَّ نِعۡمَتَهُۥ عَلَيۡكُمۡ لَعَلَّكُمۡ تَشۡكُرُونَ ۝

سورة المائدة: ٦

Legal, Social, Economic, and Humanitarian Teachings

The teachings found in the Qur'an cover many aspects of human life, they have been the subject of many publications and books, and are discussed and practiced by millions of people all over the world. There are laws covering marriage, divorce, inheritance, contracts, bearing witness, and testimonials. Civil and criminal laws, as well as advice and instructions on morality and human relations, are also present, as are systems for the equal taxation of all people, including non-Muslims. It covers many aspects of human psychology. Instructions from the Qur'an have been adopted by many nations and by many people who live in nations that do not recognize the Qur'an. Qur'anic teachings are applicable to all times and, over time, seem to prove their value as more people adopt their principles, at times without even being aware of this fact. Sometimes, man-made laws are difficult to adapt to a changing society.

CHAPTER 8

CONCLUSION

It is true that the Qur'an is not a book of science. It is also true that when one addresses a child, one has to speak in a manner that a child's brain can understand. In other words, a child is not lied to but rather is given information in a manner that is comprehensible to him. Similarly, when God addresses man in a book of teaching, He has to touch on some of the scientific aspects that are present in the surrounding environment. This is how various scientific phenomena and facts are presented in the Qur'an. The inhabitants of seventh-century Arabia could not appreciate their meaning, and it is possible that man will have to wait for a much longer time to understand the significance of all these words or statements, some of which have been discussed in this book.

The Qur'an states that time, far from being absolute, is variable in different parts of the universe. In other words, it introduces the idea of relativity. A day with God is eternal, as He is the first, the last, and the light of the heavens and the earth. He uses the term "day" in order to give the periods of the creation of the universe. In some estimates, the days of creation are calculated in terms of billions and billions of years of man's counting. He gave other examples to show that a day in other parts of the universe could be shorter. Examples of fifty thousand years and one thousand years were given. Thus, the relativity of time cannot be disputed.

Scientific evidence has shown that space is not empty. According to quantum mechanics, it contains virtual particles and anti-particles that are constantly materializing in pairs, separating, coming together again, and eventually annihilating each other. God has mentioned that He created everything in pairs. A virtual particle, according to quantum mechanics, is a particle that cannot be detected directly but whose existence does have measurable effects. Quantum mechanics differs from the general theory of relativity by asserting that particles do not have well-defined positions and velocities but are represented by a wave. It then gives laws for the evolution of a wave with time. Thus, if one knows the wave at one time, it can be calculated at any other time. The unpredictable random element comes in only when one tries to interpret a wave in terms of the particles' positions and velocities.

Astronomical observations show that the space of outer space and nebulae contains rarefied matter consisting of about 99 percent gas and 1 percent dust or, in other words, smoke. God said that the heavens and the earth were created first in the form of smoke and that, later on, He separated them. Astronomers have been puzzled over the origin of the planets. The solar system was once thought to be a rare or even unique creation. However, it is now thought that planetary systems around stars are common. Planets have been formed from the huge cloud that produced the central star: the sun. The original clouds would have consisted mainly of hydrogen, the most abundant element in the universe. Stars, like the sun, act as large furnaces that produce helium from hydrogen protons. The energy produced within these stars is so great that it may play a role in the formation of the atoms found in other elements from the original hydrogen atoms. Space is but a sea of virtual particles and anti-particles containing an abundance of hydrogen, the "element maker," from which the elements of water could be produced. This may explain God's statement that His throne, as well as His strength and authority, was "upon the water."

As God said, the earth was part of the heavens, and He separated them. This would not seem to contradict the current theory of Earth's origin. God said that the heavens and the earth possess diameters, an assertion confirmed by modern science, which suggests that they are either oval or ball-shaped. However, as the Arabic word for diameter (*aqtār*) could also mean "regions," one has to take this explanation with great reservation until new scientific evidence is produced.

He fashioned the heavens into concentric layers and placed one above the other. The lowest, to which the earth is exposed, was designed to support life on this planet. It provides markers for navigation, a source of light during the day and night, as well as sufficient heat and energy for all creatures. It also provides the basis for mathematics and calendars. Without the lower heavens and its facilities, life could never have appeared on this planet.

He created Earth and fashioned it into layers in a manner similar to that of the heavens. As our planet's interior is full of intensely hot molten rock and metals, He covered it with plates (the lithosphere). However, He left them separate from each other and caused them to resemble the bones of a human skull. These plates float on the planet's surface and are in continuous motion. The science dealing with the study of these plates is known as plate tectonics. The motions at the edges of these plates may take one of three forms. At the sites where the earth is expanding, namely, on the bottom of the ocean floor along a distance of approximately 80,000 kms., molten rock erupts from inside it and expands the affected area from 1 to 7 cms. per year. This geological phenomenon is known as "oceanic ridges." The second option, that of the edges being destroyed by sliding under the edge of the opposite plate, is called the subduction zone. If this process were to happen continually to a plate bearing a continent, all life on the planet would have disappeared eventually. However, God did not allow this to happen, for He placed mountain ranges on the opposite edge of the subduction zone. These ranges act as wedges to assure that one plate will not slide under the other and be destroyed. The third option is where the plate is neither extended nor destroyed.

As explained earlier, these plates carry the continents and oceans. God uses the word *rawāsī* (lithosphere) in the Qur'an to refer to these plates, for they are immense, were placed on the planet's surface, and were created "lest the earth would cave from under us." This is an accurate description of the lithosphere. God mentioned that He created the mountains as pegs in order to describe their function at the subduction zone. He mentioned both mountains and *rawāsī* in one sentence to show that they are not synonymous (the first is used as a noun, and the second as a verb in the past tense). It is also stated in the Qur'an that mountains were "berthed," that God is always extending the planet Earth (perhaps referring to such areas as oceanic ridges), and that He is reducing the earth from its extremities (probably at the subduction zones). The sequence of plate tectonics was not given, but it seems that the "berthing" of the mountains was the final stage.

He also related the sequence of how He is going to demolish Earth in the reverse order of its creation: He will remove the mountains, which will cause them to run away before they ultimately explode and vanish and, as a result, allow the lithosphere to move freely. The lithosphere's edges will protrude, the heat will escape from the planet's core, and the oceans will boil. Modern science has recorded runaway mountains near Frank, Canada (1903) and Mount St Helen's, Washington State, USA (1980.) The mountains ran 10-100 times their height and travelled at speeds of up to 70-120 mph. The existence of runaway mountains and landslides has been proven in Hawaii, and the phenomenon that causes them is believed to occur somewhere in the world once every decade. Scientists in Hawaii are observing, with concern and anxiety, the Great Crack that divides the main island, for the internal pressure of its magma threatens to separate the southern part of the island along this fissure. If this occurs, according to one scientist, it could cause a cascade of earthquakes and tidal waves that would have an unknown effect on human civilization.

God asked us to reflect on how He erected the mountains through a process of uplifting. In fault block mountains, a block of land is forced upward between faults. Upwarped mountains result from compression leading that leads, in turn, to uplifting part of the planet's crust. Fold mountains result from horizontal pressure that buckles rock layers into folds and then uplifts them to form mountains.

Unlike the surface of other planets, God fashioned Earth's surface by a grinding action known as *daḥāhā,* which involves the use of natural phenomena, to make life on earth possible. He provided all types of plants and created rivers for fresh water to ensure life. He protected the fresh water rivers from salty water oceans via the river estuary system. God has described the water cycle on Earth: the transportation of heavy-laden clouds by various types of wind, the precipitation of the resulting water landing on the soil, and the infiltration of the same water into the earth, where it lodges as groundwater and comes out as springs. These could form an oasis or be the source of a river. Rivers flow into the sea, but the latter's salt water does not back flow into the rivers.

He created over one million different types of animals, each of which is a nation sharing the same language. Their lives and that of man are inseparable, and in many ways man depends upon them and imitates their techniques. Some hear with their feet and receive incoming messages in a brain located in their waist. Others have scanning picture tubes in their eyes that are similar to television cameras, while still others produce light that is more efficient than man-made lightbulbs. Others can fly at 200 mph. Man invented submarines to live underwater like fish and airplanes to fly like birds. It is a well-known fact that the designer of the Spitfire, which helped to win the Battle of Britain, took his design ideas from his observations of seagulls. He was the first to design an airplane body almost in one piece. Although many animals are used as food, God ordered man to sacrifice them according to a special holy ritual. Animals will be resurrected on the Day of Judgment and perhaps will have the chance to lodge complaints against those who ill-treated them. God prohibited the use of certain meats and other parts of animals to safeguard people from serious diseases.

God created angels as obedient subjects that carry out His commands throughout the universe. Some of their duties deal with human affairs in this life and in the life to come. Interest in angels has recently become more prominent. In an American national poll, 69 percent of Americans believe in angels and 32 percent of these claimed to have had a personal encounter with them. The Devil and the jinn are made of fire. The Devil and some of the jinn carry the torch of evil in the world. As the Devil disobeyed God when He commanded the angels and jinn to kneel to man, he was thrown out of heaven. For this reason, man and his descendants became the Devil's first enemy. Supernatural powers were given to the prophets to establish their authority and as a sign of their genuine message from God. However, there are other merciful, knowledgeable servants of God that carry out His commands.

God created man, one of the wonders of His creation, from mud and then blew from His spirit into this mud. This is the energy that gave life to Adam and to all of his descendants. It seems that every bit of that energy was labeled and recognized for every man and woman. God called it before all humans came into existence to witness that He is the Creator and then sent it all back to flow through Adam's descendants.

The Qur'an describes human embryology as it is understood by modern science. It starts with a drop of semen of "mixed fluids" from the testicle, epidedymus, and prostate. This is placed in a "deep secure place" (the peritoneal cavity) and continues to develop until it reaches the state of 'alaqah, which corresponds to the blastocyst. This is implanted at the end of the first week of pregnancy and is completed by the second week. God has explained that He creates the bones first, corresponding to the notorcord that develops early in the third week and is the origin of the vertebral column around which the axial skeleton forms. At first, the embryo will simply increase in size and be in the form of a "chewed-up flesh." It takes on form during the stage of morphogenesis. The human embryo develops inside "three darknesses," which correspond to the three fetal membranes (the amnion, the chorion, and the decidua).

While man is in the womb, God "images" him in the shape of His choice and makes the right half a mirror image of the left half. Magnetic Resonance Imaging may explain how this takes place. From the very beginning God makes everybody different through the structure of DNA. Everybody is given a specific genetic code with an identical genetic map in every cell. This fact is used in DNA fingerprinting, a technique that is used in forensic medicine and parity disputes.

The importance of diagnosing pregnancy for parity and inheritance purposes also received attention from God. Hence, He allows remarriage for a divorcee only after 12 weeks and for a widow only after 17 to 18 weeks, advises breastfeeding in order to avoid gastroenteritis and other diseases in children, and advises man to use pure rain water for personal hygiene and drinking,

The gifts of sight and hearing are easily appreciated when one sees people who are born without these or other senses. He gave man a heart that initiates all electric impulses that cascade the electricity coursing through the human body. The human brain, which is more complex than a computer, differentiates human beings from animals. The power of God in creation is also illustrated by the facts that every individual has a unique set of fingerprints and that he will be resurrected with these same finger-prints. This would not be surprising, as He labeled the atoms, as well as all their particles, and keeps all of this information in a register.

The limitations of human beings are exposed in his fears and other aspects of his psychology. His spirit is allowed to roam during his sleep and wanders in the future or the past. Dreams are seen in code and can be under-stood only by those who have the necessary knowledge. Healthy sexual intercourse is seriously emphasized, although the relationship between a man and a woman is based on love, mercy, and comfort in order to ensure a happy and healthy family life.

Bibliography

Al Bar, M. A. "The Three Veils Of Darkness." *The Islamic World Medical Journal* 2, no. 2 (1986): 54-56.

Born, Irene, *The Born-Einstein Letters: Correspondence between Albert Einstein and Max and Hedwig Born with Commentaries by Max Born*. The Macmillan Press, Ltd., 1971.

Brown, B. H. and R. H. Smallwood. *Medical Physics and Physiological Measurements*. Blackwell Scientific Publications, 1981.

Clark, Ronald W. *Einstein: His Life and Times*. London: Hodder and Stoughton, 1979.

Coomaraswamy, A. K. *The Treatise of al-Jarazi on Automata*. Boston: 1924.

Einstein, Albert. *The Meaning of Relativity*. 4th ed. London: Methuen & Co., Ltd., 1950.

Encyclopedia Britannica, Vol. 4 ("Clocks, Watches and Sundails"); Vol. 9 ("Time"), and Vol. 18 ("Time"). 1978.

Hill, D. *The Book of Knowledge of Ingenious Mechanical Devices*. Boston: Dordrecht, 1974.

Llewellyn-Jones, D. *Fundamentals of Obstetrics and Gynaecology*. 5th ed. Vol. 1: *Obstetrics*. Faber & Faber, 1990.

Moore, Keith L. and T. V. N. Persaud. *The Developing Human: Clinical Orientated Embryology*. 5th ed. W. B. Saunders Co., 1993.

Stephen, Leslie. *History of English Thought in the Eighteenth Century*. 2d ed. London: Smith, Elder & Co., 1881.

Newton, Isaac. *The Mathematical Principles of Natural Philosophy*. Trans. by A. Mott. Vol. 2 (including the laws of the moon's motion according to gravity). London: 1729.

Poincaré, Henri. "The Present State and the Future of Mathematical Physics." *Bulletin of Science and Mathematics*, No. 28 (1904): 302-23.

Sabbagh, K. *The Living Body*. Macdonald & Co., 1984.

Stark, David D. and William G. Bradley, Jr. *Magnetic Resonance Imaging*. 2d. ed., Vol. 1. Mosby Year Book Inc., 1991.

The Columbia-Viking Desk Encyclopedia. Macdonald.

The Hutchinson Multimedia Encyclopedia 1995 (CD ROM). Attica and Helicon.

Whitrow, G. H. *Einstein: The Man and His Achieviement*. London: BBC, 1967.

Whittaker, Edmund Taylor. *A History of the Theories of Aether and Electricity*. London: 1953.